COULD YOU FALL AWAY?

By the same author (with Peter Lewis & Roy Clements):
Chosen for Good

Could You Fall Away?

GREG HASLAM

KINGSWAY PUBLICATIONS
EASTBOURNE

First published 1988

Front cover photo: The Image Bank

British Library Cataloguing in Publication Data

Haslam, Greg
Could you fall away?
1. Christian doctrine. Free will & predestination
I. Title
234′.9

ISBN 0-86065-494-X

Printed in Great Britain for
KINGSWAY PUBLICATIONS LTD
Lottbridge Drove, Eastbourne, E. Sussex BN23 6NT by
Richard Clay Ltd, Bungay, Suffolk.
Typeset by CST, Eastbourne, E. Sussex.

Contents

Introduction

Bob was my room-mate in my first year at college. We were both away from home and excited by what lay ahead for us. Although very different from each other in temperament, personality and background, a friendship grew between us, and Bob became increasingly more interested in my Christian faith. The week before we all went home for Christmas he had prayed to receive Christ with many tears and much joy. By the following summer, however, he was a mess. His life was on the rocks, mainly through alcohol. Any talk of the Lord was an embarrassment to him. He was involved in a tragic accident and became embittered towards life in general, and Christianity in particular. The glow had gone. The Lord was no longer real. His profession of faith had evaporated. That was fourteen years ago and, as far as I know, he has not recovered the faith he once so enthusiastically confessed.

Mo and her husband Doug were just about the keenest young married couple we had in the church. They used their home very much for the Lord and had both enjoyed a great deal of his presence and power since they came to him and fell in love with each other some years before. Mo asked the most perceptive questions in our weekly studies in 'Romans' and together they seemed likely to prove to be a tremendous asset to the church as the years went on. Within two years, however, Mo had formed an adulterous relationship with a colleague at work, left her husband and given up all interest and involvement in Christian things. Eight years on we have lost all contact with her and, from a purely human perspective, there doesn't seem any way that we shall ever see her take up her profession of being a Christian again.

These two stories—both true—could be repeated among the friends and acquaintances of most Christians who have had the sad experience of watching apparently keen Christians begin drifting and then depart completely, or so it seems, from all connections with vital Christianity.

You may have picked up this book because you know of someone who has abandoned the faith in just this way, but it's probably more likely that your real reason is one of fear for yourself. You may have been disturbed by such cases, both in real life, and as they occur here and there in the pages of Scripture. Perhaps you've been alarmed by the warnings contained in such passages as Hebrews 6:4–6 and Hebrews 10:26–31, and wondered very seriously if they would ever prove true of you. You may even believe that you have actually been guilty of the terrible sins described there. For still others, the reason for picking up a book of this kind is a real desire to avoid such a fall.

My aim then has been to help people like you. This book is a serious attempt to look carefully at the two above-mentioned passages, and to explore whatever other scriptures we can find which shed light upon the ugly subject of backsliding and apostasy. At the same time we will look together at many of the vivid narratives in Scripture concerned with men and women who either fell away completely from the faith, or who came very close. All of this should help to remove misunderstandings and confusion in our thinking and, above all, act as a spur to press on vigorously in our walk with the Lord.

The story is told of a wealthy and aristocratic lady in

England who was looking for a chauffeur to drive her new Rolls Royce. She interviewed a number of men, posing each one the same problem, and then pressed for an answer. Near her home the roadway bordered dangerously close to a steep cliff with a fall of several hundred feet to the rocks below. She asked each driver how near to the edge he could safely drive. The first answered, 'Oh, probably about five or six feet, Ma'am, with no difficulty at all.' He was immediately dismissed as unsuitable for the job. In an endeavour to impress her Ladyship, the second would-be chauffeur ventured to say, 'I think I could drive within eighteen inches of the cliff edge, Ma'am, and never have an accident.' But to his total bewilderment he too was dismissed as unsuitable, just as the first had been. When the same question was put to the third man, his reply went something like this, 'Ma'am, with such a precious cargo as your good self aboard, I would keep as far away from the edge as I possibly could.' He got the job.

This book, then, has not been written merely to excite curiosity as to what lies over the edge of departure from Christ, and certainly not to cause anyone to stumble further towards that edge. It has been written in order to show you how precious you are to God and how marvellous is the work he has done in your life. It has been written to give you the incentive to stay as far away from 'the edge' as possible and to press on into all that God has for you.

And if you are reading this book because you are away from the Lord and in danger of giving up altogether, then my prayer is that you will hear from the Lord who loves you and receive a fresh touch of his Holy Spirit, bringing you back to your first love (Rev 2:4–5).

Part One:

The Teaching of Hebrews

I

The Most Troubling Passage in the Bible?

We are going to start at the deep end. We will begin with those terrible passages that seem to have caused such trouble to so many genuine believers. They portray a sin so dreadful that we shudder to see it described. Moreover, the passages seem to imply that it is authentic believers who may commit this sin and, to compound our terror, the words pronounce such awful judgement on them that there seems no likelihood of recovery or forgiveness. Here are the verses in question:

> It is impossible for those who have once been enlightened, who have tasted the heavenly gift, who have shared in the Holy Spirit, who have tasted the goodness of the word of God and the powers of the coming age, if they fall away, to be brought back to repentance, because to their loss they are crucifying the Son of God all over again and subjecting him to public disgrace (Heb 6:4–6).

> If we deliberately keep on sinning after we have received the knowledge of the truth, no sacrifice for sins is left, but only a fearful expectation of judgment and of raging fire that will consume the enemies of God. Anyone who rejected the law of Moses died without mercy on the testimony of two or three witnesses. How much more severely do you think a man deserves to be punished who has trampled the Son of God

> under foot, who has treated as an unholy thing the blood of the convenant that sanctified him, and who has insulted the Spirit of grace? For we know him who said, 'It is mine to avenge, I will repay,' and again, 'The Lord will judge his people.' It is a dreadful thing to fall into the hands of the living God (Heb 10:26–31).

You can see the problems immediately. These verses raise enormous questions in our minds. Most of us, either the moment we became Christians or very soon after, came to some kind of certainty or assurance that we had eternal life. Friends, booklets and above all the Bible affirmed confidently that 'eternal' meant everlasting, that Jesus would never let us go, and that our future was now secure. Not even death could snuff out the life God had given to us. The eternal future was ours in God's new heaven and earth!

So what about all this dreadful talk of 'falling away'? Who could do such a thing? And how could they do it, given all that the Lord has done for them? Can I personally lose my salvation if such a fall is a reality? Can I fall so as never to recover, and if so what becomes of the *eternal* life I once possessed?

These are big questions. Any pastor will tell you that he's been asked more than once about these verses, and not in a detached or academic way, but by troubled Christians, often plagued with doubts and attacks upon their assurance arising directly from these verses. One very experienced and tremendously gifted teacher of God's people, the late Dr D. M. Lloyd-Jones, Minister of Westminster Chapel, London, for some thirty-eight years, has said concerning these verses:

> I can say definitely after some 35 years of pastoral experience that there are no passages in the whole of scripture which have more frequently troubled people and caused them soul agony than the passage in Hebrews 6:4–8, and the corresponding passage in Hebrews 10:26–29. Large numbers of Christian people are held in bondage by Satan owing to a misunderstanding of these particular statements.[1]

It appears that these verses have been a problem to every generation of Christians. In the earliest centuries of the Christian church, particularly as the church became further and further removed from the assuring teaching on grace taught by the first Apostles, a kind of moralism crept in. These words began to produce great alarm among believers. In the second and third centuries AD there came a tendency to emphasize the believer's good works as the primary basis of assurance. The dilemma came when some of those believers fell, often quite badly, into such sins as adultery or idolatry. Then, as now, there was enormous pressure from an immoral society to cause Christians to indulge in sexual sins. Furthermore, waves of state persecution so threatened and terrified these Christians that it seemed a light thing to some for them to burn incense to the spirit of Caesar as a god if that action could deliver them from pain or even death. The question was: Did such sins seriously jeopardize a person's salvation, or perhaps even place them beyond the possibility of salvation for ever? Here were examples of a kind of 'fall' from the faith which could not but be viewed very seriously indeed.

It was frequently asserted that such a 'fall' is the sin described in Hebrews 6:6, and that once a person has been initiated into the Christian faith by baptism (which they equated with the phrase 'once been enlightened' in Hebrews 6:4), if they were ever guilty of such a lapse then there was no hope of forgiveness. It was this kind of thinking which caused the first Christian Emperor, Constantine, to postpone his baptism until he was on his death bed! He didn't trust himself not to sin again had he been baptized earlier.

You can see the problem. For you too, no doubt, have the memory of many 'falls' since you became a Christian and perhaps some of them have been very serious. Have you lost or forfeited your salvation because of them? And even if God grants us another chance on this kind of basis, how many 'chances' does God give us? Does there come a point when he says, 'Enough! That person is now apostate. There is no more possibility of repentance or forgiveness for them. They must await my judgement.'?

Those who teach that assurance rests on the basis of faith in Christ alone frequently affirm that these verses definitely teach the possibility of real Christians falling away for ever. Many serious students of Scripture are convinced that Hebrews 6 and 10 are the death blow to the Calvinistic teaching that the saints will persevere, or be preserved by God, right through to the end. They discredit the 'once saved always saved' outlook and assert as an alternative the very real possibility of being saved and lost. They believe that all the phrases in Hebrews 6 describing those who fall away apply to none other than a truly born-again Christian.

Here 'once enlightened' would remind us of such a passage as 2 Corinthians 4:6—'For God, who said, "Let light shine out of darkness," made his light shine in our hearts to give us the light of the knowledge of the glory of God in the face of Jesus Christ.' As this describes the experience of all true Christians, what can the person depicted in Hebrews 6 be, other than a true Christian? 'Who have shared in the Holy Spirit' seems as clear as day. This surely points to an indwelling of the Holy Spirit which is the privilege only of true believers (Rom 8:9; 1 Cor 6:19)? Similarly, 'tasted the heavenly gift' (Heb 6:4) can only mean that they have received into their innermost being the gift of salvation.

'Tasted the good word of God' is surely a possibility only for a real Christian? For if, as Paul says, 'the man without the Spirit does not accept the things that come from the Spirit of God, for they are foolishness to him, and he cannot understand them, because they are spiritually discerned', then for a person to 'taste God's word' and to find it 'good', it must be the case that the Spirit of God has worked a great change in such a man—the change we call conversion.

So also '[tasted] the powers of the coming age' must mean that they have been given a foretaste, a sampling here on earth of the future state in heaven when we shall live in resurrected bodies having passed through trials and judgements. The believer's privilege now is to live in a measure of victory over sin and to enjoy the blessings of walking with God, which we will know fully only when eternity breaks in and the eternal age dawns.

Now Hebrews 10 is briefer in its description. It simply talks of those who have 'received the knowledge of truth' (v.26), but what could be plainer? As the nineteenth-century preacher R. W. Dale expressed it:

> I know not how he (the writer to the Hebrews) could have chosen expressions which more forcibly describe the possession of a real and genuine Christian life. Phrase is heaped upon phrase that there may be no misapprehension.

And since the passage in Hebrews 6 goes on to speak of how it is impossible for such people to be 'brought back to repentance' and Hebrews 10 leaves them the prospect only of 'a fearful expectation of judgement and of a raging fire that will consume the enemies of God' (v.27), the conclusion seems unavoidable: the Bible is asserting that true Christians can fall away or, in short, that they can be saved and subsequently lost.

But if this is so, it alerts us to certain problems. What of Jesus' promises as our Shepherd to give eternal life such that 'they shall never perish; no-one can snatch them out of my hand' (Jn 10:28), and the Apostle Paul's glowing assurance at the end of Romans 8 that nothing 'will be able to separate us from the love of God that is in Christ Jesus our Lord' (see Romans 8:31–37)? Is the Bible contradicting itself? And what does Hebrews 6 actually assert? Will it accommodate the subsequent return of the person guilty of the sins which it describes?

Most advocates of a 'saved and lost' view of the

Christian life teach that the door by which we exit from the state of being saved is a revolving door, and that backsliders do return. Apostates do come back, and so a person can re-emerge from a state of being lost into a state of salvation once again. But if Hebrews 6 teaches that we can be saved and then lost, then it also denies the possibility of our being saved all over again through fulfilling certain conditions. It says emphatically and without qualification that 'it is impossible' for such people to be 'brought back to repentance' (vv.4,6). Therefore we must understand it in its broadest sense: it is impossible for them to repent, impossible for Christian friends to bring about their repentance, and impossible even for God to restore them. If this view is correct, then what Hebrews 6 teaches is terrible to behold. It asserts the possibility of some people, who have once been saved, falling away and thus being lost for ever.

The inability to see that the people described here could be anything other than true Christians, and the equal inability to see how a Christian could lose his or her salvation has led some Bible teachers to propound the view that what is given here is a serious but *hypothetical* warning. It couldn't actually happen, but it is there in vivid technicolour to show the *logical consequences* of drifting away from the Lord or of backsliding in the Christian life. Such people need to know that if they fall away then their sin would be unforgivable. Thus it is a warning in the strongest terms, like the bright red lightning fork painted at the foot of some electricity pylons, or the open jaws of a fearsome shark painted on signboards at some beaches off the Australian or Californian coast; they warn of what might happen *if* some foolish person trespassed up that structure or into that water, but of course no one would be foolish enough to do so. And so, much is made of the little word 'if' at the beginning of Hebrews 6:6, 'If they then fall away.'

That prince of preachers, Charles Haddon Spurgeon,

forcefully brings home the thrust of this particular viewpoint in a sermon preached in 1856. As he describes this 'falling away' he says:

> There never has been a case of it yet; therefore I cannot describe it for you by observation; but I will tell you what I suppose it is. To fall away would be for the Holy Spirit to go entirely out of a man — for His grace entirely to cease; not to lie dormant but to cease to be — for God who has begun a good work, to leave off doing it entirely — to take his hand completely and entirely away and to say 'There man! I have half saved thee; now I will damn thee!' That is what falling away is . . . falling away would involve God's grace changing its living nature, God's immutability becoming variable, God's faithfulness becoming changeable, and God Himself being undeified; for all these things falling away would necessitate.[2]

Now such a possibility was unthinkable to Spurgeon, believing as he did that God's people always persevere in the faith right to the end. What he then does is to pick up on the word 'if' which appears in most translations of this verse:

> . . . if God put it in, he has put it in for wise reasons and for excellent purposes. Let me show you why. First, O Christian, it is put in to keep thee from falling away . . . it is calculated to excite fear; and this holy fear keeps the Christian from falling . . . second, it is to excite our gratitude. Christian! If thou shouldst fall away, thou couldst never be renewed unto repentance. Thank thy Lord then that he keeps thee.[3]

But the major problem with this perspective, valuable as it is, is simply that the word 'if' does not appear at all in the original Greek which has only the words 'and having fallen away' (*Kai parapesontas*), an aorist participle describing a real possibility which may already have actually happened among some of the readers.

A hypothetical warning is really no warning at all. Power-lines *do* electrocute, sharks *do* bite and that's why we take the kind of posted warning signs I mentioned earlier very seriously indeed. Who could honestly be afraid of something which could never happen? Would the Bible warn us in such a way?

The great New Testament scholar, Professor F. F. Bruce, in rejecting this hypothetical view says very plainly:

> Biblical writers (the writer to the Hebrews being no exception) are not given to the setting up of men of straw. The warning of this passage was a real warning against a real danger, a danger which is still present so long as 'an evil heart of unbelief' can result in 'falling away from the living God' (Heb 3:12).[4]

What is stated by the writer to the Hebrews is stated soberly as something that can happen, and church history and experience vouch for the fact that it has happened. People do give every appearance of being genuine Christians and yet, through one factor or another, they do fall away and renounce the Lord.

But this leaves us with great problems, the main one being understanding accurately what the writer to the Hebrews was warning against. We know that scripture cannot contradict scripture, and that the Scriptures clearly teach assurance in such a way that we are left in no doubt that we will 'make it to the end'.[5] So why would the writer address believers in this frightening way when his stated aim was to encourage them? What exactly is he warning against?

One very persuasive and attractive solution, which has been advocated by some in recent years, is that the writer has indeed described the condition of true believers in Hebrews 6:4-5, but that what is lost by the sin of 'falling away' is not salvation itself but rather the rewards which accompany salvation both in this life and in the next. There are certain privileges awaiting the believer which can only be enjoyed now by a steady and consistent walk with God. The writer is saying that if we fall into impurity, laziness and carnality we will forfeit the rewards God gives to those who are pure, diligent and spiritual.[6]

All of this is, of course, beyond dispute. Such passages as 1 Corinthians 3:12–15 speak of the believers' works being tested in order to determine their rewards. The prospect of reward motivated the Apostle Paul greatly in his indefatigable labours for the Lord (2 Cor 5:9–10), and the Bible's teaching on assurance in no way warrants slackness, laziness and indifference in living the Christian life.

But helpful as this view is, it seems to fall far short of an adequate description of what Hebrews 6 and 10 are really speaking about. There, both the actual sin and its consequences are far more terrible than the shame and dishonour brought to the Lord by Christians frequently living way below par, and the disgrace many will face at the judgement seat of Christ when they realize that they have forfeited their rewards.

Remember, the sin described is one of 'crucifying the Son of God all over again', 'subjecting him to public disgrace', 'keeping on sinning', 'trampling the Son of God underfoot', 'treating as an unholy thing the blood of the covenant that sanctified him', and 'insulting the spirit of grace'.

The punishment threatened is the impossibility of being 'brought back to repentance' (Heb 6:6), 'being cursed' and 'burned' (6:8) with the same fire that will 'consume the enemies of God' (10:26). The loss here is more than the rewards of salvation—it is salvation itself. The sin here is more than backsliding—it is to say farewell to the Lord and his Spirit for ever; to renounce Christianity in a high-handed and wilful manner.

It is to this view of this passage we will turn in the next chapter.

2

The Unforgivable Sin?

In looking at these very difficult verses from Hebrews, which we have called 'the most troubling passage in the Bible', we have seen that there are various ways of understanding their meaning, none of which is completely satisfactory. We have also realised how important it is to understand the nature and the consequences of the sin described before we ask soberly, 'Who could do such a thing?'

The sin being described is more serious than the dangerous drifting and even backsliding which so many Christians fall into, in that it is no less than a complete falling away from Christianity.

The phrase in Hebrews 6:6, 'If they fall away,' uses the past participle of the Greek verb *piptein* which means 'to fall headlong, to fall absolutely'. A striking example of another occurrence of this verb is in Romans 11:11 where the Apostle Paul is discussing the almost wholesale rejection of Jesus as Messiah which characterized his fellow Jews in their response to the gospel. He goes on to assert his confidence that this is only a temporary season of unbelief on the part of the Jews, and that one day they will turn to the Lord and believe the gospel in large numbers. He begins this assertion by asking this question concerning his fellow Jews, 'Again I ask, Did they stumble so as to fall beyond recovery?'

For our purposes, what is intensely relevant about this question is the way Paul uses two different verbs. The first, translated 'stumble', is from the Greek verb *ptaiō,* but the second, translated 'fall beyond recovery', is from the verb *piptein* which occurs in Hebrews 6. Paul says here in Romans that his fellow Jews have fallen badly, yes, but they have not yet come as far as to 'fall beyond recovery'. This distinction is important.

In the Christian life you can fall many times, and some of those falls will be bad ones. Christians have been known to lapse into all the sins of the flesh—drunkenness, lying, theft and sexual immorality to name just a few. And yet, shameful and contradictory of our position in Christ as these sins are, they are not the 'fall beyond recovery' or 'falling away' spoken of in Hebrews 6. The latter is a fall so serious that there remains no possibility of forgiveness, restoration, repentance or recovery. Peter denied knowing Jesus in an act of cowardice under persecution. David fell into adultery and murder when he took Uriah's wife, Bathsheba. Dreadful though these sins are, they do not amount to the 'falling away' described in Hebrews 6, for both Peter and David were gloriously brought back to repentance. They were also forgiven and restored, a state which Hebrews 6 says would be *impossible* for the kind of sinner he has in mind.

What is this sin then? To answer that question we must first remind ourselves how it is described in the other verses which follow. It is called 'crucifying the Son of God all over again and subjecting him to public disgrace' (Heb 6:6). It is also compared to rejecting the law of Moses (10:28), and further depicted as trampling the Son of God under foot, treating as an unholy thing the blood of the convenant and insulting the Spirit of grace (10:29). These phrases express succinctly the whole of Christianity in its bare essentials and the reaction of certain wicked people to it. They speak of the Person of Christ, his atoning and saving death on the cross, and the gracious work of the Holy Spirit in bringing us to faith in Jesus and his death. ('The Son of God', 'the blood of the covenant', 'the Spirit of grace'.)

So what was this wicked reaction? Surely it can be none other than a complete renunciation of Christianity. It is an avowed and deliberate severing of all links with Christianity and a return to one's former irreligious or false religious background in full awareness of the issues. Some people have done this only secretly or mentally because it has served their interests to go on being known as a 'churchman' or 'nominal Christian' in their public life. But whether this denial of the faith was open and public or a private decision in the person's own mind, they went ahead with their vile sin even though they clearly knew what they were doing. Such a renunciation is so complete that we may say that those people will remain impenitent about it to their dying day. They have 'fallen beyond recovery'. They have not simply backslidden, but have committed the terrible sin of apostasy. Having completely severed their links with Christ and his saving death, and utterly repudiated the convincing ministry of the Holy Spirit, nothing more can be done for them. Nothing can save them. They are lost for ever. 'It is impossible for those . . . if they fall away, to be brought back to repentance' (Heb 6:4,6).

Such people are beyond recovery for the reasons the writer to the Hebrews gives us. First, *'they are crucifying the Son of God all over again'*, meaning that they approve of all that the Jewish mob and the governing body of Judaism did to Jesus from Gethsemane onwards. They say, 'Yes, Jesus is guilty as charged.' They wish he was dead. They cast their votes against him. They scream passionately, 'Crucify him! Crucify him!' in a bid to rid their lives of his influence. They would hammer the nails in again and rejoice at his death were it to be repeated before their gloating eyes. They would dance on Jesus' grave if they could. How can such a rejection of Jesus' death ever be forgiven since Jesus' death is the only means of forgiveness?

Secondly, they are *'subjecting him to public disgrace'*. They are identifying with that same mob that pummelled Jesus' face with angry fists, that spat on him, plucked tufts of hair from his beard and decked him in the mock robes of royalty in sarcastic laughter and derision at what they considered his totally false claims to be a prophet or a king. Such people are saying in effect, 'We've tried your Christianity . . . stuff and nonsense! It's all a hoax, a pack of lies, a total deception. We spit on Jesus and the Bible as worthless rubbish to be refused and rejected as garbage.'

Thirdly, they have *'trampled the Son of God under foot'*, stepping carelessly and lightly over Jesus' person and work as no longer worthy of their consideration. They talk of his bones rotting in a Palestinian grave—that is, if he ever existed! They smirk with contempt at our worship and our life submission to him as Lord, thinking that we insult their intelligence if we expect them to believe such rubbish.

Fourthly, they have *'treated as an unholy thing the blood of the covenant'*. The saving power of Jesus' death and the cleansing potency of his blood now seems to be childish Sunday school sentiment at best and 'butcher-shop' theology and the 'gospel of the shambles' at worst. It irritates them to hear that God ordained the death of Jesus to avert his wrath and make possible his forgiveness of sinners. These apostates say that such a message should be avoided as unworthy of consideration—they treat it as an 'unholy thing'.

Fifthly, they have *'insulted the Spirit of grace'*. They resist all his convincing work and shake off every one of his convictions. They call it all 'emotionalism' and 'sinister brainwashing'. They laugh when they see others moved to tears. They attribute genuine conviction and repentance in others to the 'manipulative pressurizing of those charlatan evangelists'. Zeal for the Lord is 'religious mania and dangerous fanaticism'. The Holy Spirit does not exist. His work is a fiction, his miracles a fraud which only the gullible and brain-damaged would be foolish enough to believe.

And what makes this cumulative rejection of Christianity so unforgivable, and therefore so final, is that it is committed by people who do not act in this way out of ignorance,[7] but rather out of a full understanding of what they are doing. They are turning away from the only means by which God's mercy could flow down to them, and resisting in hard-hearted blasphemy the only one who could convince them of the truths they now vehemently deny—the Holy Spirit.

You can see why this sin is unforgivable, and why it would be 'impossible to restore them to repentance'. What more could you say or do to convince such a person? Is there any new information you could give them which would touch their hard hearts or tip the scales of their impenitence the other way? There is not. Is there any factor of truth you could introduce which would unlock the tumblers of their steel-hard unbelief? There is not.

That this is not hypothetical is vouched for by the facts which emerge from both Scripture and church history. These records are strewn with the wrecks of those who have committed this sin. We shall consider one or two scriptural examples later.

But now some vitally important questions remain: Who could do such a thing? And more importantly: Could a Christian ever be guilty of such a sin? And to make this even more personal to any Christian reading these verses, we must ask this question: Could *you* fall away?

To answer these questions we must ask who the writer to the Hebrews envisaged as potential candidates for this dreadful sin.

3
How Could They Do It?

The letter to the Hebrews has been shrouded in many mysteries even to this day, as Bible scholars have sought to understand accurately its message and its relevance to the church. Since its author chose to remain anonymous, we don't know who wrote it. Since its readers are never precisely designated, we don't know exactly for whom it was intended. And since the situation in which it was originally received is not explicitly defined, we don't know exactly what pressures its readers were living under. But a consensus of opinion has emerged.

It was written by a leading apostolic figure (possibly but probably not Paul) with an active ministry among, a comprehensive acquaintance with, and a fervent compassion for his own kinsmen by race, the Jews. It was written before the destruction of the Temple in AD 70 to a converted readership of believing Jews, during that interim period when Judaism enjoyed a considerable amount of legal protection within the Roman Empire and Christianity was manifesting its true colours, both to Jews and Gentiles, as a major new force in the Empire. Christianity could no longer be identified merely as a sect within Judaism or a cult to be easily accommodated by the tolerant, easy-going religious policy of Rome.

For those believing Jews, life was proving increasingly difficult. They had recognized in Jesus the long-promised and awaited Messiah and come to faith in his death by crucifixion as the fulfilment of the sacrificial system dating from Moses. After a marvellously enthusiastic and courageous beginning to their new-found and deeply-satisfying faith, they were coming under tremendous pressure to compromise and even abandon their profession of Jesus as Lord. This pressure came from two sources.

First, the pagan world and, more particularly, the Roman authorities increasingly came to regard Christianity as a troublesome pestilence in its refusal to affirm Caesar's lordship alongside that of Christ's. Christianity was seditious and could no longer be afforded the privileges accorded to Judaism as a *religio licita* within the Empire. It must be stamped out.

Secondly, the claims of Jesus, and more particularly his ignominious death on the cross as a tried and proven enemy of the people, all demonstrated conclusively to the Jews that he was a blasphemer and charlatan of the first order, and died as he deserved, hanging under God's curse on the 'tree' (Deut 21:23) of a Roman gibbet.

Therefore, for a Jew to become a Christian was an act of double-jeopardy. He forfeited the legal protection which he had once enjoyed from the Roman state in the religion of his forefathers. More seriously still, he bore the stigma of being charged as a rebel and a blasphemer by his fellow Jews. They would take no time at all to point out the new disciple's 'losses' in becoming a Christian. He had lost the Temple with its rich sacrificial system and its ministry of properly called and ordained priests who could represent his needs to God and mediate God's provisions to meet those needs. He had chosen to follow a worthless deceiver, Jesus of Nazareth, and had thrown in his lot with a despised bunch of 'no goods' and 'no hopers' in the Christian church. For such vile folly and loss of integrity he could expect only the derision and contempt of his fellow Jews, a contempt which at times broke out in open abuse, mob violence, arrest without trial, and the plunder of his property (Heb 10:32-34).

It's easy to see, then, that many of the original readers of this epistle would have been hovering undecidedly in the halfway house of a frozen and fearful halting between two opinions. As Jews, some would have been seriously considering the step of total identification with Christ and his people and already have received instruction in Christian truth in order to come to an informed decision. As the pressure mounted they would be sorely tempted to give the whole thing up and return to the fold of the older, more familiar Judaism. Others, like them, would possess a very clear idea of the fundamentals of this new faith and in fact would have come to a decisive commitment to Christ and identification with his people in baptism. But under the strain of the enormous pressure I have described, they would have been seriously wondering whether a life of discipleship and costly commitment to Christ was for them.

The writer to the Hebrews addressed this 'mixed audience' of readers in an epistle which he calls 'a short word of exhortation' and which is interspersed at various points with dire warnings of the consequences of retreating from Christ into the retrograde step of a return to Judaism. To all intents and purposes he assumes that all his readers were converted, but he wishes to warn them solemnly that a return to Judaism is a denial of Christ. For them to do this knowingly would be to commit apostasy; it would be unforgivable, for no real excuse could be extended to account for such a lapse. A fall as serious as that would expose such a one for his true standing with God and lay his life open to the inevitable judgement of God, a judgement far more terrible than the hardships mere men can inflict.

Hebrews 6, therefore, gives us a description of the kind of people most in danger of such a fall. We return to the five phrases which some have seen as a conclusive description of a Christian in order to try to understand properly the state of the persons they describe.

These people have *once been enlightened*. 'Once' indicates that this experience had really happened to them. This, along with the other four experiences, was a genuine operation of the Holy Spirit and came upon them because of their growing acquaintance with Christianity. In order to explain this phrase, it is helpful to turn to a verse like 2 Corinthians 4:4—'The god of this age has blinded the minds of unbelievers, so that they cannot see the light of the gospel of the glory of Christ, who is the image of God.' This demonstrates conclusively that to be enlightened means nothing more or less than to see and understand who Jesus is. Paul's assertion that Satan blinds unbelievers' minds, and that he does so in all men without exception, must mean that the Holy Spirit, using the truth of God's word, penetrates that darkness and removes that ignorance.

The point I wish to make here is that it is possible to have one's ignorance about Jesus removed and yet to fall short of true new birth and full conversion. We can be tremendously impressed listening to a sermon, we can feel that 'the penny dropped' and 'at last I see it' and to an extent we are right. But this may only be the essential precursor to salvation—not salvation itself. People who 'know the right answers' and are clear on the fundamentals of the faith are enlightened and very privileged. But this does not mean that they are yet converted, as any Sunday school teacher or Bible class leader will tell you. Clear understanding doesn't spell total commitment.

E. W. Johnson, an American Bible teacher, has expressed this distinction very memorably: 'All who have been regenerated have been illuminated [i.e. enlightened]. But not all who have been illuminated have been regenerated.' To know and even enjoy Christian doctrine is no evidence of conversion. It may be a delight only to the intellect, stimulated by the logic, majesty and awesome reality of biblical truth. So while 'being enlightened' is the ongoing privilege of truly born-again Christians (Eph 1:18, 2 Tim 1:10), it also denotes that coming to a 'knowledge of the truth' (Heb 10:26), which *must* occur in anyone in order for true conversion to take place, does not, in and of itself, constitute true conversion. Something more than that is needed. As 2 Corinthians 3:18 asserts, the knowledge of Christ which is truly converting is one that causes us to go on 'being transformed into his likeness with ever-increasing glory, which comes from the Lord, who is the Spirit'. In other words, it is a reception of the truth that totally renews our nature and goes on progressively changing it to resemble and reflect Jesus' character.

Secondly, they are said to have *tasted the heavenly gift.* The 'gift' in question is not explained, but could mean a number of things in connection with salvation. It could mean God's saving power (as in Ephesians 2:8-9), or the person of Jesus (as in John 4:10), or more likely the Holy Spirit himself (as in Acts 2:38, 8:20 and 10:45). It's best to give the word as wide a meaning as possible, for what he has in mind is that these people are in no unclear position as to the reality of God and his salvation, for they have 'tasted' it.

Some expositors insist that the verb 'tasted' means nothing less than 'fully experienced' God's salvation, for it is the verb used of Jesus in Hebrews 2:9 when he is said to have 'suffered death, so that by the grace of God he might taste death for everyone'. It must certainly mean 'experienced to the full' there. Others have agreed that it amounts to no more than merely 'trying' something, for the same verb occurs in Matthew 27:34 when Jesus tasted the wine and gall-drugged mixture offered to him on the cross, but refused to drink it. He sipped the contents, but refused to imbibe it fully and take in its full effects. This second meaning is surely what the writer had in mind, for he is describing people who have 'sipped' but refused to 'drink', who have 'tasted' but fallen short of 'eating and digesting' God's gift of salvation.

Isn't it perfectly possible to be in the position spiritually where you admire Christ, listen avidly to preaching, join in all the songs exulting in God's deliverance for his people, feel in a measure excited by the whole uplifting business and yet at the end of the day never press on to submit your life to Christ at all? This is exactly Jesus' complaint to the crowds of hangers-on (mostly pursuing full bellies and exciting miracles) in John 6:36, 'You have seen me and still you do not believe.' What all this amounts to is an experience of Christ which renders a person without excuse for his subsequent act of denying and renouncing him completely.

Thirdly, the most difficult phrase of the five, they have *shared in the Holy Spirit.* As we agreed earlier, only true believers are indwelt by the Holy Spirit (John 14:17; Rom 8:9; 1 Cor 6:19). But is that what the writer has in mind? There are other ways in which we can partake of the Holy Spirit which fall short of his actually indwelling us, and therefore fall short of salvation. What I mean is this. The Holy Spirit can operate *on* the lives of those *in whom* he never takes up permanent habitation. The verb here, *metochous,* means literally 'to hold with' the Holy Spirit. It is to co-operate with the Holy Spirit in some way, such that one can act as his partner in some of his workings.

Now this may be controversial to some, but it seems clear from Scripture that the Holy Spirit can operate his gifts, or something very much like them, even in unconverted people. Those operations are meant to be seen in the lives of the members of his church, the body of Christ (1 Cor 12, Rom 12), but if God could use Balaam's ass to speak to the wayward prophet, then he can take up and use unconverted men to prophesy, to heal or to do some mighty work. This may only be an occasional or temporary operation, but it is real nevertheless. Consider carefully Jesus' solemn prediction that at the Judgement

Day many will protest their right to enter heaven with: 'Did we not prophesy in your name, and in your name drive out demons and perform many miracles?' Our Lord would not dispute this fact—but he will still say finally to them, 'I never knew you. Away from me, you evildoers!' (Mt 7:22–23).

Paul said it is possible to operate in gifts and yet be devoid of God's love—a contradiction which only confirms the hollowness and vacuous emptiness of such a 'charismatic' imitation of the Spirit's full work (1 Cor 13:1-3). Such an anomaly is possible, but is not God's idea of what it is to be truly charismatic. That is why functioning in some operation of the Spirit is not a guarantee that a person is even saved, let alone filled with the Spirit. Judas operated in most of the gifts (Mt 10:1-8), albeit only temporarily, yet Jesus was later to call him the 'one doomed to destruction' in John 17:12.

So it is possible to 'share in the Holy Spirit', that is to partner the Holy Spirit in some of his gifts and operations, and yet not be truly saved at all. Caiaphas, the high priest who pursued Jesus to the dreadful death of the cross, was taken up and used to prophesy something of the meaning of Jesus' death (Jn 11:49-52). This passage of Scripture says that he did not do this 'on his own', and so by clear implication the Holy Spirit was involved, yet he was a lost man. He 'shared in the Holy Spirit', but was ultimately lost.

As we follow this line of thinking we can see that the fourth and fifth features must be understood similarly. They have *tasted the goodness of the word of God.* Here 'word' is the Greek *rhema,* which almost invariably denotes the spoken or preached word of God, as it is used in Scripture. What is being described here is all too common. Hundreds of people pass through our churches to become affected to one degree or another by the word of God spoken powerfully into their lives and yet, sadly, they leave as they came—unconverted people.

They admired the preacher, felt gripped by his message and on occasion were even moved to tears. They saw themselves described in those prophetic messages and could only say of what they heard that it was 'good'. Such preaching has rendered them without excuse on the Judgement Day, but they have now gone from our midst and were never converted. How do we know that? In the words of the Apostle John,

> They went out from us, but they did not really belong to us. For if they had belonged to us, they would have remained with us; but their going showed that none of them belonged to us (1 Jn 2:19).

Finally, in saying that they had tasted the *powers of the coming age* he means that they even personally experienced something of the miraculous in their lives. The 'coming age' or the 'age to come' is this gospel age running roughly from Christ's ascension around AD 30 to his second coming, we know not when. (Read Joel 2:28–32. It is quoted as now fulfilled, by Peter, in his sermon in Acts 2:16–21.) In Mark 16:15–18 Jesus said that these gifts, signs and wonders would characterize the whole of the gospel age, and certainly the writer to the Hebrews could say without dispute that his readers had seen such miracles themselves and known that they had happened to confirm the truth of the gospel message which they had heard (Heb 2:3–4)—a fact which would make 'ignoring' such a salvation so much more inexcusable (Heb 2:3).

The thrust of all that we are saying is this: it is dreadfully, frighteningly possible for someone to come very near to salvation and yet ultimately to fall short of it by denying and suppressing all the work of God they have seen and felt in other lives, in the preaching they have heard and in the ways they themselves have been touched and used by the Spirit of God even to the point of seeing conclusive miracles. Such people may go on to deny vehemently the whole business and renounce adamantly their involvement in Christianity for ever.

In the medical sciences the principle of immunization entails the practice of giving someone a mild dose of a certain infection or disease in order to inoculate them against the real thing. Many people experience just enough of Christianity to inoculate them for ever from 'catching' the real thing. They eventually prove by their conduct and their words that they have rejected all they have seen and no longer want any part in it. They 'fall away' completely from their involvement. They become apostates who return to their former irreligious life, or in the case of the readers of Hebrews, the false religion of Judaism which rejects Jesus as the Christ and persecutes his people.

This was the danger in which so many of these readers stood. They were drifting (Heb 2:1) and in danger of falling victim to a sinful, unbelieving heart (Heb 3:12). They were refusing to press on in the Lord and so stood in imminent danger of going back.

To do so would be to commit apostasy and demonstrate that they were never really Christians in the first place. This danger is not hypothetical; it is real. The sustained thrust of the writer's message is: make sure that none of you ever falls in this way; don't go back, go on (Heb 6:1–3). For, to use his own illustration, it is possible to receive the same blessings which others receive, just as adjacent fields receive the same rain and sunshine in the summer seasons of growth. Yet one ground produces wheat, the other only thorns and thistles. The fault doesn't lie in the rain, it lies in the ground (Heb 6:7–8). Such ground is worthless. The blessing of rain hasn't changed the character or true nature of the ground, so, true to its own character, it can only produce thorns and thistles.

This reminds us of a similar passage in 2 Peter 2 which has caused the same kind of debate we've been engaged in here. It says of the wicked false teachers who deny the

Lord that they 'have known the way of righteousness' but now 'turn their backs on [it]' (v.21) and so fulfil the proverbs: 'A dog returns to its own vomit,' and, 'A sow that is washed goes back to her wallowing in the mud' (v.22). Their temporary 'conversion' to Christianity and subsequent renunciation of it demonstrated conclusively that though the 'dog' had been domesticated for a while, and the 'sow' scrubbed and bedecked in a ribbon, they remained unchanged in their nature and now acted true to their character as unconverted 'dogs' and 'swine'.

Such is the seriousness of apostasy. It proves that person was never converted. More solemnly still, it puts them in the position where they never will be converted, for as we have said, what more could be said or done to a person who had experienced so much, yet thrown it all aside as worthless? There is 'a sin unto death' (1 Jn 5:16–17) beyond which there is no point in praying for the guilty party. Hebrews 6 describes that sin. Do you think you could commit it? If you are truly converted you could not. If you are presently backsliding, you cannot be so sure.

It is to these issues of true conversion and the state of clouded assurance, which almost invariably shroud the hearts of those who are dangerously drifting due to backsliding, that we now turn.

4
How Can I Be Sure?

Amid all these serious warnings to his readers, the writer seems to have had an underlying confidence that each of them would press on with God and shun the sin of apostasy, moving on to a full commitment and faithful following of Jesus as true Messiah, Saviour and Lord.

But one thing should now be clear; his confidence in them, and our confidence in ourselves, does not lie in the fact that the five phrases of Hebrews 6:4–6 can describe us accurately. They could all be true of us and yet we could still fall away. On what basis, then, is true assurance grounded?

In answering that question we will look at a very helpful division used by older writers on the theme of assurance. It is based upon the Apostle John's words in 1 John 5:7–8—'For there are three that testify: the Spirit, the water and the blood; and the three are in agreement.'

Assurance of our firm standing in Christ is based on the saving death of Jesus on the cross ('the blood'), the transforming effects this has already had upon us in cleaning out our lives ('the water'), and the inward witness of the Holy Spirit giving a solid sense of certainty as to our standing by his powerful work in our hearts and on our lips ('the Spirit').

We pick up these themes as the writer to the Hebrews himself handles them in 6:9–20 and elsewhere:

> Even though we speak like this, dear friends, we are confident of better things in your case—things that accompany salvation. God is not unjust; he will not forget your work and the love you have shown him as you have helped his people and continue to help them. We want each of you to show this same diligence to the very end, in order to make your hope sure. We do not want you to become lazy, but to imitate those who through faith and patience inherit what has been promised. When God made his promise to Abraham, since there was no-one greater for him to swear by, he swore by himself, saying, 'I will surely bless you and give you many descendants.' And so after waiting patiently, Abraham received what was promised. Men swear by someone greater than themselves, and the oath confirms what is said and puts an end to all arguments. Because God wanted to make the unchanging nature of his purpose very clear to the heirs of what was promised, he confirmed it with an oath. God did this so that, by two unchangeable things in which it is impossible for God to lie, we who have fled to take hold of the hope offered to us may be greatly encouraged. We have this hope as an anchor for the soul, firm and secure. It enters the inner sanctuary behind the curtain, where Jesus, who went before us, has entered on our behalf. He has become a high priest for ever, in the order of Melchizedek.

He says in effect in verse 9, even though I have spoken so solemnly and seriously of the dreadful sin of apostasy in verses 4–8, I am convinced that these things will not prove to be true of you, and that you will all evidence and demonstrate true salvation in Christ.

The witness of the water

In looking for the basis of such certainty we must see first the way in which he describes the *character* of his readers. They truly demonstrate the transforming power of the gospel in their lives. In verses 17–18 they are described as 'heirs of what was promised'. Heirs inherit their riches not by works but by relationship. They know what it is to receive by free gift and donation. Do you? Have you actually accepted it?

They are also said to have 'fled to take hold of the hope offered to us'. This describes an active response to the gospel. They have heard the offer and not sat passively by, nodding approval of its wonderful terms (as so many do in evangelistic meetings). Rather, they've actively *fled* or run to God to accept it as their own possession.

This outgoing trust or believing confidence in God has issued in tremendous and conscious changes within them. They are said to be in the condition where they now *love God:* 'The love you have shown him' (literally love shown 'to the name of him', *eis to onoma autou*) (v.10). They love everything God has shown himself to be; each person of the trinity—Father, Son and Holy Spirit; each attribute of his character—his justice as well as his love.

They also *love God's people*—'You have helped his people and continue to help them' (v.10). The love of which he speaks is actually a strong cord of many strands which binds us to the family of God. It includes valuing and esteeming them: you see how precious each of them is to God and you view them as he does, bought very expensively with Christ's blood. You enjoy being with them: to you they are the best company in the world, and you can't think of anyone you'd rather be with. They are both your family and your best friends, therefore you find yourself wanting to serve them and promote their good. You give to them, visit them, and spend time speaking encouragingly to them. You lend books to help them, pursue them if they're slipping downhill, put their reactions before your own 'rights' as you consider a course of conduct, and generally put yourself out to show a love that is earthed and practical.

These, then, are some of the 'things that accompany salvation'. If you are truly saved there will be a new love for God and a new love for God's people consciously present in your mind, your outlook and your lifestyle. (See Hebrews 10:32–34 where the same conduct is reiterated as evidence of their true standing as believers.)

The fact that God 'will not forget' such conduct (6:10) means that it is not irrelevant in determining one's true standing before God. This is true throughout Scripture.

Romans 5:1–5 urges us to possess peace with God but affirms that this is bolstered as a consciously enjoyed experience when we see evidence of God at work in us as we endure trials, persevere through them, and develop tested character.

Similarly, the first epistle of John has often been subtitled by expositors 'The Tests of Life' because of its emphasis, in an almost matter of fact way, on the realities which will inevitably be found in any true believer's life. He 'does what is right' (2:29), 'purifies himself' (3:3), breaks with sinful habits (3:6), loves his brother (3:14) and overcomes the enticements of the fallen world (5:5), to name just a few of John's assertions in this epistle.

The witness of the blood

But a new character and lifestyle are not all that evidence true conversion. More importantly, it is also determined by the stance we take towards Christ, both to his person and the work he performed for us on the cross. The writer has already discussed Jesus' total supremacy over angels, since he is the Son of God (chapter 1), and also his superiority even to the great heroes of Israel like Moses and Joshua. These men worked as servants in God's household of salvation as it was being built in space and time, but Jesus himself is the builder! He leads us into a better 'land' than Joshua ever did (chapters 3 and 4). Furthermore, Jesus was both offering and great High Priest who gave up his own life when he 'tasted death for every man' and made our total rescue from sin not only a possibility but a reality (chapters 2 and 5), in his death upon the cross.

This message has come as a promise and an oath to us, just as it did to Abraham whom the Bible considers to be the 'Father of all who believe' (Rom 4:1,11). Here in Hebrews 6, Abraham is said to have modelled or exemplified the appropriate response to God's message which came as 'a promise confirmed by an oath'. Verse 16 says an oath 'puts an end to all argument'. The gospel is meant to put an end to all debates and disputes about your eternal destiny and it will do so if, like Abraham, you simply believe it.

Do you accept that Jesus is totally supreme, that he is Lord? Do you trust him to bring you to God as your Priest, one who has made a clear yet bloodstained way back to God by his own death on the cross? Then this is enough, for this is faith.

But many doubting believers often ask, 'What is faith?' and, 'How can I be sure I've really got it?' Faith involves three things: knowledge, persuasion and trust. *Knowledge* because it first hears and understands the message by the enlightening work of the Holy Spirit: 'Faith comes from hearing the message, and the message is heard from the word of Christ' (Rom 10:17). True faith is always based upon content. There is a minimum content a person must know concerning who Jesus is and what he has done if they are to be saved. But as we have seen from Hebrews 6:4, merely being enlightened is not enough, and if this process of coming to faith halts there, then true faith is aborted and the life is extinguished: we are still-born. The 'live birth' of true faith contains two more ingredients.

In addition to knowledge, faith moves on to become *persuasion*. Abraham was 'fully persuaded' of the truth of what God had spoken to him (Rom 4:21). His arguments were demolished, his doubts were removed. He was convinced of the reality of unseen things by a supernatural persuasion of God's Holy Spirit. Do you find within you a

Spirit-given certainty that Jesus' death on the cross was so potent that it can save you, and that his resurrection from the dead was so real that he can speak life into you and totally rescue you from sin and Satan, from death and hell? Where did that certainty come from? What is it? It is Spirit-given *faith.*

Such persuasion always issues in *trust.* Trust means total self-commitment, the reorientation of one's life, one's expectations, one's choices and one's outlook. Abraham expected God to keep his word, and learned to wait patiently (Heb 6:15). He put his life on the line and became the possessor of a faith that was fixed in his heart and which enabled him to persevere and press on in all God had said to him until he inherited what God had promised. If you've got trust you can't abandon it. You'll 'imitate those who through faith and patience inherit what has been promised' (Heb 6:12). You'll 'take hold of the hope offered' and *never* let it go. You'll be 'anchored' to Jesus, and whatever storms hit the battered boat of your life you'll never drift away completely (Heb 6:19–20), for faith holds on to Jesus who, as our great High Priest, holds on to us with a grip which can never let us go (Heb 6:20; Jn 10:28–29).

The writer to the Hebrews is only interested in a faith which perseveres, for that is the only kind of faith worth having. In Hebrews 10:37–39 he quotes from the prophet Habakkuk the words of the Lord, 'But my righteous one will live by faith.' Habakkuk spoke these words concerning a people who would undergo a long trial of oppression by the Babylonians. Some of those suffering Jews would have abandoned the faith or would 'shrink back' as verse 38 puts it. But others would endure, and stay close to God. How? By faith! For faith is a persevering trust as well as a settled conviction.

And so Hebrews 10 closes with a glowing statement of confidence which the writer is sure applies both to himself and to his readers: 'We are not of those who shrink back and are destroyed, but of those who believe and are saved.' He then spends a whole chapter (Heb 11) unfolding the true nature of faith. As we have seen already, it is both a *settled persuasion* (Hebrews 11:1, 'Now faith is being sure of what we hope for and certain of what we do not see') and also a *persevering trust* (Hebrews 11:4–40, and the glorious examples of men like Abel, Noah, Abraham, Joseph, Moses and the rest).

His main point is that a true believer cannot fall away or apostatize. He doesn't abandon the truth under any circumstances. He holds on tenaciously through persecution, mockery, apparent delay, buffeting at the world's hands, torture and even death. You can see the relevance of all this to both his original readers and also to us. Is that the kind of faith you've got? Then be assured, you wouldn't have it if you were not a Christian. If you're a Christian you have only one option: it is not going back, it is going on.

The witness of the Spirit

In all of this there is radiating through the inner man, or heart, of every true believer the clear voice and witness of the Holy Spirit who produces in us a *cry* and a *confession,* that is, an assured speaking of the lips which flows from the convinced condition of our hearts. The *cry* is in Romans 8:15–16, 'You received the Spirit of sonship. And by him we cry, "*Abba,* Father." The Spirit himself testifies with our spirit that we are God's children.'

Before you were converted you felt like an orphan in the world. Children without natural fathers miss out a great deal. Some become maladjusted even to the degree of becoming social misfits or sexual deviants. Similarly, without a sense of God's fatherhood our lives are out of joint. We become drifters, directionless and hopeless. We become angry and estranged, insecure and bewildered both towards people and towards our environment. But upon true conversion and experiencing the anointing of the fullness of God's Spirit in our lives, we become clearly conscious that we now have a *Father*. We just *know* it. It's almost our first and truest instinct as a new-born child of the God who is there.

When visiting Israel some years back, I was touched to hear young Israeli children shout 'Abba' to their fathers in a number of significant circumstances—through tears of pain due to a fall on the rocks, when lost in a crowded supermarket, when thirsty under the scorching midday sun. Here is the cry of respectful, filial confidence. Someone loves me! Someone cares! Someone I can trust has my total welfare at heart! Not one of those trusting cries for help went unanswered.

But these are the same kind of convictions and cries the Holy Spirit produces within true believers. We too are enabled to cry out loud, 'Abba, Father!', and we know he is! We are sure he cares for us because he is the God who is really there!

The *confession* is in 1 Corinthians 12:3 and Romans 10:9, 'No-one can say, "Jesus is Lord," except by the Holy Spirit,' and, 'If you confess with your mouth, "Jesus is Lord" . . . you will be saved.'

Is Jesus the boss in your life? Are you unashamed to let it be known that he is? Unembarrassed to speak of your allegiance to him before men? Glad to sing, say, preach and declare 'Jesus is Lord' in an unforced way on each appropriate occasion? Does this flow as a clear and resounding certainty from your heart to your lips?

If the answer is 'yes' to each of these questions then you must be a Christian, for the indwelling Holy Spirit produced that confession and, as we've discovered, he only indwells true Christians. If you have got this clear confession of Jesus' lordship in your heart then you are not, nor ever could be, an apostate, for you are a Christian.

This threefold assurance clouded

So the Spirit, the water and the blood all testify to our true standing in right relationship with God. But why does this assurance so often become clouded in the lives of even true believers? And why do we so often take to ourselves the warnings of Hebrews 6 and 10, concluding that they describe our present condition when 'better things' should really be true in our case? Why is it that we sometimes fear for our salvation and wonder about ourselves, spending so much time and energy questioning and being anxious about our security in Christ?

Surely it is because we have 'drifted' (Heb 2:1) into a similar condition to that of the original recipients of this letter. We have, through laziness or pressure, intellectual problems or ignorance, cowardice or even retreat, lapsed into that dangerous 'no man's land' where we are no longer truly pressing on, and where, *to all appearances,* we look like we're seriously considering turning back. In short we are *backsliding.* We will look at this dangerous condition in detail later, for it is this condition which lands a person on the slippery slope and in the halfway house where to others, and even to himself, he may become totally indistinguishable from the potential apostate.

But first, we are going to see Jesus' own masterly corroboration of these stark realities as we consider two of his parables. Both of them indicate that it is possible to make some profession of faith, get involved in the church, and be indistinguishable from true Christians for a while, and yet ultimately prove to be lost. Both of them also point us in the direction of understanding accurately the nature of true conversion.

Part Two:

The Teaching of Jesus

5
Are You a Good Catch?

> 'Once again, the kingdom of heaven is like a net that was let down into the lake and caught all kinds of fish. When it was full, the fishermen pulled it up on the shore. Then they sat down and collected the good fish in baskets, but threw the bad away. This is how it will be at the end of the age. The angels will come and separate the wicked from the righteous and throw them into the fiery furnace, where there will be weeping and gnashing of teeth.' 'Have you understood all these things?' Jesus asked (Mt 13:47–51).

When I was a student at Durham University I recall arriving for the start of a new term to find the Students' Union and refectory liberally plastered with posters advertising free trips to the USA for adventurous and open-minded young people. My enthusiasm for such a trip was considerably dampened, however, when I discovered that the posters had been displayed by Rev. Sun Myung Moon's Unification Church. I'd have to become a 'Moonie' in order to benefit. The price was too high. But I wonder how many others got sucked in by this devious device, only to regret it for the rest of their lives?

As a small boy in Liverpool I was originally enticed under the influence of true Christianity because of the attraction of the sandpits and play house which were part of the furnishings in the premises of our Sunday school at that time. Once in, I was soon to loathe every minute of it and couldn't wait to get out. (I apologize for this, but this was my experience at that time.)

Many people get caught up in Christianity through surface attractions and later decide to abandon it completely. The difference here is that Christianity is not something you can safely abandon, as one might desert cults such as the Moonies or other non-Christian philosophies and suffer no adverse consequences whatsoever.

In this parable Jesus is indicating that many people become caught up with Christianity because of its great power to collect men indiscriminately. He uses the graphic picture of fishermen deploying their nets either in the salty brine of the Mediterranean or the clear, fresh waters of the Sea of Galilee. Such evangelistic endeavours on the part of his 'fishermen' will catch 'all kinds of fish' (v.47), in that people of different nationalities and social groups, of diverse levels of education and intelligence, and people of totally diverse personalities are often drawn into the sphere of influence of Jesus' kingdom.

Some arrive with *the shoal.* They love company and so if their mates go to church or a close school friend or work companion is interested, then they will be too. Some of these people may even be 'loners', drawn by the warmth, reality and down-to-earth care of Christian people. There are great attractions in moving with the crowd, especially if that crowd is a crowd of Christians.

Some arrive because of *the commotion.* For many, life is a bore. When the excitements of the 'A' Team, the disco, the race-course and the fairground begin to pall they may give this 'interesting new church' a try. A net full of attractive exciting fish may be a draw to other fish, and so bored people are drawn out of curiosity. They simply want to see what all the fuss is about.

Some are drawn by *the bait.* They sense the enjoyment, intellectual stimulus and sheer delight which God's truth and God's presence bring to the minds and hearts of God's people and they want 'a piece of the action' too. It may be that a broken marriage, a guilty conscience or the fear of hell draws some of these 'fish', attracted by the evident peace and security offered to God's people.

But the truth is that however good the apparent size of the catch might be, Jesus here warns us that not all who come within the orbit of Christianity are truly converted to Christ. There's a mixture of *good* fish and *bad*—'When it was full, the fishermen pulled it up on the shore. Then they sat down and collected the good fish in baskets, but threw the bad away' (v.48).

Many people protest against coming to church because, as they say, 'the church is full of hypocrites'. Here is a surprising fact which such people need to know— they aren't the first to talk like that. Jesus said it long before them and here anticipated that the presence of hypocrites in his church would always be an ongoing condition of her gathering together until he returns. It is a compliment to Christianity that people expect its adherents to be perfect straight away. It's just too bad that they will always be disappointed.

Isn't it true, therefore, that people often profess Christianity and stay among truly converted people for less than the best reasons? As the glow of a light bulb on a warm summer's evening will attract ugly moths and bugs, so the light and life of God's presence among his people will draw others to that light, people who may never be lastingly affected by it. Many will soon be changed, but others will hang around indefinitely with no radical change of heart or life. They will go on experiencing the superficial pleasures of being near to the light, yet draw the line at allowing that light to penetrate deep down into their beings with its transforming power.

It is perfectly possible that the devil sends some of them. In the similar parable of the weeds, Jesus has the farmer say of those noxious stalks of darnel planted surreptitiously amid his precious crop, 'An enemy has done this' (Mt 13:28). The devil infiltrates churches as he did the circle of Jesus' twelve disciples with his own 'plants' or fifth columnists who are there to water down our testimony and ultimately disgrace Christ and his church by their inevitable apostasy which will take place sooner or later.

What Jesus makes clear, in both this and the earlier parable of the weeds, is that premature separation is impossible. Men cannot do it properly or infallibly, in that they would end up throwing out the wheat with the weeds or frightening all the good fish away as well as the bad. It's only when the net is finally pulled in that the true condition of the fish will be revealed. This should alert us to the fact that those who will ultimately prove to be apostates are largely 'faceless' people. We cannot recognize them for the simple reason that they look like the real thing. It is much more important then, that we put these tests alongside our *own* lives, rather than go around sizing up all the members of our church to see if they're potential apostates. This latter task just cannot be done.

Yes, some members *are* hypocrites, play actors, pretending to realities of which they really know little or nothing at all. But we can never judge by superficial appearances. We can't read hearts. If you heard a twenty-stone man lecturing on dieting you might angrily dismiss him as not worth listening to. 'The man's a hypocrite!' you'd say in contempt. But what if only six months beforehand he'd weighed thirty stone, and was still losing weight? That's not hypocrisy, that's progress! People look at the church's imperfections and don't realize that every life within it is still under construction and not yet finished. That doesn't make the people hypocrites; it just means they're not perfect yet.

Sadly, we must conclude that some of those people are not under construction, they're under condemnation. They are pretending to a faith they do not possess. They stand in danger of complete apostasy. Such people may only be revealed at the Judgement. They are 'bad fish' and their unfitness to be among God's people will be exposed one day, but that day has not yet come.

The last book of the Bible, Revelation, tells us what kind of people will be excluded. We have in mind here such verses as Revelation 21:8, 'But the cowardly, the unbelieving, the vile, the murderers, the sexually immoral, those who practise magic arts, the idolaters and all liars—their place will be in the fiery lake of burning sulphur,' and Revelation 22:15, 'Outside are the dogs, those who practise magic arts, the sexually immoral, the murderers, the idolaters and everyone who loves and practises falsehood.'

These terrifying lists are character descriptions of the natures of ungodly people, some of whom will find their way into the church under the passport of a phoney profession of faith. If we couple some of the suggestions from these lists with Jesus' fishing analogy we come up with some illuminating descriptions of such rebels and apostates.

The *fearful* remind us of those lurking, heavily camouflaged predatory fish who hide on the sea bed or amid rocks. They picture for us the barren, fruitless lives of many church people, lives indistinguishable from the world. They are fearful in that they hide their Christianity. They have no convictions they would stand for, and they fear the cost of true discipleship and commitment. They are ashamed of Jesus before men and will deny him publicly when the occasion is right to do so. They don't want God to make them brave.

The *dogs,* the next title used by the Lord in describing the wicked, strikes us as rather an unusual comparison to make when it is human beings one has in mind. This ugly metaphor is not meant to conjure up pictures of the well-groomed and obedient hounds most of us are familiar with. These mangy, diseased pariahs which scavenged the streets of ancient towns and villages were as far removed from the domesticated pets we know today as a sewer rat is from a tame white mouse in the cage in junior's bedroom. Such animals devoured the carcasses of dead animals and have their counterparts in the 'unclean fish' (see Leviticus 11:9–12) listed in the Old Testament such as crabs, shrimps and crayfish who live on death and host multitudes of dangerous bacteria by their despicable eating habits. The apostate is dead to God and finds his pleasure in deadly things like unclean films and magazines, unwholesome entertainments and unrestrained lusts. They don't want God to clean them up. Therefore, any apparent change in them is only a surface one.

Those who practise magic arts are a little difficult to tie in with our analogy. It may be stretching our analogy a little far to find examples in the 'fish world' in order to be consistent with the flow of this parable, but Deuteronomy 4:18 forbids making idols in the form of fish in order to worship them, and fish feature regularly in the ancient religious cults of Egypt and the Middle East. These are professed 'Christians' who abandon the faith for the 'greater stimulus', to their minds, of drugs, astrology, tarot, mediumistic seances, spiritism, magic, healing arts and so on. They do not want God's truth and the genuine supernaturalism of biblical Christianity.

Those who are sexually immoral are mentioned next. The list of unclean fish mentioned earlier from Leviticus includes those that don't have 'fins and scales'. Fins *and* scales would suggest perfect adaptation to their environment and no peculiarities, and by analogy in a spiritual sense would condemn human beings not adapted to the world as God made it. All forms of sexual immorality are sinful rebellion against God's absolute standards and have no place in the natural world as he ordained it, whether we speak here of heterosexual fornication and adultery, or of the homosexual perversion which those same standards prohibit. The people with unclean minds and immoral actions who willingly live in such debauchery, thinking and speaking in obscenities, reading literature and watching films which traffic in perversions, will one day awaken to the frightening realization that heaven has for ever excluded them. They refuse to be straightened out by God and so will one day be confirmed in their crookedness for ever.

The *murderers* picture for us those voracious, violent and homicidal sharks and recall to our minds the images of those people who are consistently motivated by hate, bitterness and resentment. 'Anyone who hates his brother is a murderer, and you know that no murderer has eternal life in him' (1 Jn 3:15). They are swirling reservoirs of malice living under the disguise of Christian 'brothers' and 'sisters'. They refuse to let God fill them with his love and so are doomed to join the destroyer in hell for ever.

The *idolaters* are those empty, worthless souls who are devoted to nonsense, to wasted ambitions, and to 'gods' which have no real existence. Like inedible minnows, only fit to be thrown back into the water, their lives are similarly useless. Devoted to the passing philosophies of men, their own material possessions, some fading political ideologies or even to their own appetites ('Their god is their stomach' Phil 3:19), they refuse to give God first place in their lives.

Those who love and practise falsehood are the slippery 'eels' who resemble the arch-deceiver Satan, that lying serpent. These pretenders, who may even sit at communion with God's people, are elusive, dishonest and difficult to get hold of. They are people you feel you will never know, for they are tale-spinners, liars and deceivers themselves. They don't want God to put truth into their inmost being (Ps 51:6), preferring to live a lie. But one day that lie will be exposed before the blaze of God's glory, and all such frauds will be revealed in their true colours finally and for ever.

Such is the representative list of the true characters of those who will ultimately suffer exclusion from heaven, even if they were once caught in the wide-sweeping net of the church's effective outreach as she carried out the Lord's commission to be fishers of men.

Jesus concludes the parable by enforcing the point we have repeatedly underlined concerning their inevitable and infallible exposure as mere hypocrites. The fishermen sit down to examine each fish carefully. There's nothing haphazard or distracted about this, and so not one will 'slip through the net' of this thorough examination. This is actually delineated as the task of the angels (v.49), for while such pretenders can successfully fool teachers, preachers and fellow church members, they cannot fool the Lord and his angels. Only one possible destiny awaits such people: 'The angels will come and separate the wicked from the righteous and throw them into the fiery furnace, where there will be weeping and gnashing of teeth' (Mt 13:49–50). Yes, this is the awful fate the writer to the Hebrews said would await all apostates, 'In the end the land that produces thorns will be burned' (Heb 6:8). 'A fearful expectation of judgment and of raging fire will consume the enemies of God' (Heb 10:27).

Jesus challenged all his hearers as he would challenge all today who stand in danger of committing the sin of apostasy: 'Have you understood all these things?' (Mt 13:51). For Christianity is not conveyed only sacramentally (as if mere attendance on the ordinances of baptism or communion made you a Christian), only sentimentally (through deeply moving emotional experiences such as those induced by glorious singing or dramatic and powerful preaching), or fatalistically (by passively assuming that it is enough just to be with Christian people). No, there must be the understanding hearing of Jesus' message and the response of faith we spoke of in the last chapter. For unless Jesus has penetrated your mind with his truth, persuaded your heart to believe it, and moved you to trust him, you will stay in the condition of being a dead unclean fish all your days and be rejected throughout all eternity.

So, if you are presently caught up in the net of his church, make sure that you have a right to be there. The consequences would be dreadful if you found out too late that you have no such right.

6

Conversions False and True – the Parable of the Sower

Faced with the frightening possibility of being so close to the kingdom yet finally being excluded from it, most of us need no prodding to find out from God's word how Jesus teaches us that his people are genuinely to enter the kingdom and simultaneously to let the kingdom genuinely enter them. In this, probably the most important of all Jesus' parables, the Master explains unambiguously how true conversion happens, and also shows us why false conversions frequently occur alongside them.

> That same day Jesus went out of the house and sat by the lake. Such large crowds gathered round him that he got into a boat and sat in it, while all the people stood on the shore. Then he told them many things in parables, saying: 'A farmer went out to sow his seed. As he was scattering the seed, some fell along the path, and the birds came and ate it up. Some fell on rocky places, where it did not have much soil. It sprang up quickly, because the soil was shallow. But when the sun came up, the plants were scorched, and they withered because they had no root. Other seed fell among thorns, which grew up and choked the plants. Still other seed fell on good soil, where it produced a crop – a hundred, sixty or thirty times what was sown. He who has ears, let him hear' (Mt 13:1–9).

Jesus here makes plain that the process by which his

kingdom grows is analogous to the process of seed being sown. He spoke of four types of ground upon which that seed will fall, and—shocking to realize—in its reception of the seed only *one* of those soil types is a picture of true conversion. At least two of the other receptions may look like conversion but they are not. So it is very important that we understand what kind of soil you and I as individuals represent. Are you 'good soil'?

A few words of introduction

1. Christianity expands by seed being sown

There is an affinity, a mutual suitability between human hearts and the word of God. They were made for each other. Until God's word enters into a person's life, it doesn't matter how potentially rich the soil of their heart is. It will only remain barren, black and unattractive dirt until the right seed meets it and the miracle of change and growth begins to occur. People will never know what God created them to be and they will never realize their true destiny until the word of God enters them through true conversion.

That is why God has set enormous store by the preaching of his word. Someone has said that 'God only had one Son and he made him a preacher'! This was the number one priority in Jesus' public ministry (see for example Mark 1:21; 2:2; 4:1; 6:2, 34), and therefore it must be priority number one for his people, the church today, in relation to its witness to the world.

2. The seed we sow is powerful seed

The truth is that *all* words are powerful. One political theorist said he was going to conquer the world with twenty-six lead soldiers. He meant the typeface of the printing press which published his works. It doesn't matter whether such words are words of cheering encouragement or biting sarcasm, of religious heresy or philosophical nonsense, God has ordained that words become powerful vehicles which can change the hearts, lives and destinies of men. How vital, then, that it is God's word we pass on to others.

The most powerful words are God's words. Jesus here compares them to seed which produces a return, in the right soil, of thirty, sixty or even a hundred fold. Any farmer will tell you that a return of thirty fold is a fantastic harvest, but Jesus envisages double and even more than treble that figure in some fields. We're talking powerful seed here!

Remember that, when you next pass on the word of God. Every tract is a letter bomb, every sermon a land mine, every preaching mission a barrage of big-guns because of the explosive potential of God's word.

3. Some of our sowing is apparently wasted effort

It seems a colossal waste for some of that seed to become either food for birds or to be choked by weeds and scorched by the sun. This explains why so much Christian work can be so discouraging. You teach that youth group every Friday night, or speak at that City Mission every Sunday afternoon, and so many hear but so few respond. We often feel like giving up because going on seems to be so much effort for so little result.

But Jesus wants us to know that the weakness doesn't lie in the power of the seed sown, which is *always* powerful and which therefore merits our confidence, but rather in the condition of the soil in men's hearts into which it is dropped. Also, the parable indicates that often the most immediate results are the most suspect. They may be the first to fall away! Because we have to wait a long time to harvest the fruits of our labour doesn't mean that God is not at work. He is. Be patient. 'Your labour in the Lord is not in vain' (1 Cor 15:58).

Now, turning to the heart of the parable itself, we will

look at the significance of the four responses which Jesus describes.

The pathway—the 'flash-in-the-pan' conversion

This, of course, is no conversion at all.

> As he was scattering the seed, some fell along the path, and the birds came and ate it up ... When anyone hears the message about the kingdom and does not understand it, the evil one comes and snatches away what was sown in his heart (Mt 13:4, 19).

This is the response, if we can call it that, of the totally unthinking soul as he hears the word of God. This person is not even 'enlightened' in the sense we have discussed in Hebrews 6:4. There is a firm and unyielding resistance to the word.

In Eastern farms there were few boundaries to the fields, so travellers followed well-worn footpaths which criss-crossed the farmland at various points. On those pathways the soil was beaten down hard by the sandals of thousands of seasonal foot-sloggers. The farmer's sowing was not the accurate, machine-assisted affair it is today. It was done by hand in a wide sweeping movement of the farmer's arm. Inevitably some of the seed would hit these foot-rollered pathways. At those points this tempting 'bird-table' set out by the hands of the benevolent farmer would prove irresistible to the birds. As soon as it was conveniently safe they would swoop to fill their bellies with the surface seed lying so temptingly upon the hardened pathway.

In our churches, there are hearers who may have the sounds of God's word hitting their eardrums but that is the sum total of the effect. They are no different to the seats they are sitting on in terms of their response to the word. They are there most Sundays and if we pressed them for more their response would be: 'What more do you want?'

Age, familiarity or the tough experiences of life may have hardened them, and they consistently refuse to hear the word, no matter how lively, novel or interesting the presentation. They simply switch off when the preacher begins. The seed never gets a chance to lodge, so Satan's birds snatch it away as quickly as it falls. It is, as we say, 'In one ear and out of the other.'

Too many distracting footsteps have beaten over the footpaths of their minds, and amid the traffic of newspapers, gossip columns, soap operas, music lyrics, human opinions and other crowding thoughts, God's word is a mere noise not worthy of their attention. Since their hearts present a smooth unploughed surface unable to receive the word, there is no real reception. Such is the pathway.

The rocky ground—the 'shallow' conversion

> Some fell on rocky places, where it did not have much soil. It sprang up quickly, because the soil was shallow. But when the sun came up, the plants were scorched, and they withered because they had no root . . . [This] is the man who hears the word and at once receives it with joy. But since he has no root, he lasts only a short time. When trouble or persecution comes because of the word, he quickly falls away (Mt 13:5–6, 20–21).

This is not simply soil with a few rocks in it, it is a thin layer of top-soil covering some horizontal strata of limestone just an inch or two beneath the surface. Pity the seed which lands there! Of course, there is some kind of germination. As the roots push down so the lush green shoots rise up and break the surface to become visible, for a while, above ground.

It's not long, however, before the rainy season is over and the long Palestinian summer issues in months of scorching heat as the sun climbs daily overhead. The seed begins to wither and die because it is absolutely parched of water. Unable to dive any deeper for precious moisture, both roots and shoots become desiccated and die in no time at all.

So it is with all 'shallow' conversions. Initially there is every appearance of faith after exposure to the gospel. At their first church service or special outreach, or after some time of encounter with Christians, or perhaps after reading the scriptures or Christian fiction, the person's response is very encouraging. Having decided to follow Christ, he can't wait to pass his sincerely-held opinions on to his Christian friend: 'Wow! Yes! Terrific! Never heard anything like it! That's for me! Count me in! I've never felt so happy in my life! How come nobody told me this before? When can I join the church? Get baptised? Sure, anything you want. Hey, this is wonderful!'

Before long he's giving his testimony, getting involved in the church's activities, and generally fitting in well with the rest of his new circle of Christian friends. But in due time the tragedy is that this 'convert' who went up like a rocket begins to come down like a burned-out stick.

Jesus makes it clear that the missing ingredient is that no one explained the cost of following him. Sooner or later trouble hits this blazing ball of zealous enthusiasm like a hose pipe of cold water under pressure. The flames of his zeal are quickly doused with the suffocating effects of adversity and persecution.

Instead of congratulations all round, he's met with sarcastic derision at work. Far from winning friends and influencing people, he's losing old mates like someone who's developed a problem with personal hygiene! Worse than this, he hits difficulties even in the church. Someone offends him with one or two careless remarks, and that girl he's met in the young people's fellowship has lost interest and gone after somebody else.

Why is it that nothing seems to have gone right since he became a Christian? He was overlooked for promotion, the dog was killed in a road accident, and the car blew a head gasket. Doesn't God care? Sceptical questions dart from his wounded heart like spines from a porcupine's back. He's on the retreat and the defensive. And there seems to be no let up in the unexpected pressures he is now facing.

Before long he's concluded, 'This new way of life isn't for me after all.' He's like those unthinking recruits who join the army because the advertisements promised them travel, adventure, a macho uniform to impress the girls, and endless opportunities for the display of their latent heroism. Nobody mentioned the sergeant major and the 5.00 am call-out to the parade ground, or the route-march (in full battledress) through fifteen miles of icy mud and howling-cold northerly winds. At the first scent of trouble he goes AWOL (Absent Without Leave!).

Will he be back? Possibly not. His mild dose of Christianity has served only to inoculate him against the real thing. His hot fever of early enthusiasm has given way to the sustained chill of total indifference. Here is an example of what C. T. Studd called 'The Chocolate Soldier'.

We must be clear about this. Jesus didn't die in ignominious shame, soul torment and agony on the cross to make 'chocolate soldiers' of his disciples. He died to capture our hearts, our wills, and our total allegiance and to turn us into people who know how to triumph in adversity and persevere through all the hardships which men or devils can throw at us.

The shallow convert in his total lack of conviction, courage, stability and perseverance demonstrates that he was no true convert at all. He may have fooled many, but his departure from the Lord, his apostasy from the faith, exposes the true character of his heart. Under the surface layer of top soil is a soul as hard as rock to the love and grace of Christ—a soul that remains unbroken and impenitent under this message of a crucified Saviour and his call to follow him unconditionally.

The thorny ground—the strangled conversion

> Other seed fell among thorns, which grew up and choked the plants ... [this] is the man who hears the word, but worries of this life and the deceitfulness of wealth choke it, making it unfruitful (Mt 13:7, 22).

Like the previous 'convert', this person gives every appearance of being a genuine Christian for quite some time. But this is not really the case. In his heart other permanent residents of an unsavoury kind remain undisturbed and sooner or later begin to threaten the effectiveness of God's word and, indeed, do so right from its first implantation.

Yet the presence of these thorns and thistles may not be obvious at first. There are some things which are suppressed, or which a person wouldn't think of doing in the first flush of awakened religious feelings when God is very present and the seed of his word is being powerfully sown. In this ground there may be a high degree of illumination which penetrates much more deeply than in the previous ground. If this soil had the potential to grow thorns, it also had the potential to produce a good crop of wheat had it not at the same time been contaminated with these alien competitors for its attention.

So, as we have seen with the rocky ground, the heart of such a person has not been totally won to the Lord. This person loves God *and* Mammon (see Matthew 6:24), and Mammon will win every time unless the grace of God roots out that tenacious weed and frees the soil to realize its proper potential. Other obnoxious plants compete with the growth of God's word. A slow process of strangulation sets in. The man's love for material things is expressed in a preoccupied anxiety for such concerns as his job, his pay, his house, his car, his savings, his holidays, his ambitions and his security.

He begins to lead something of a double life. He indulges in entertainments and practices he would refrain from if other Christians were with him. He goes to places he'd be quite embarrassed to be spotted attending. He's hankering for the old life and lifestyle. He thinks he's missing out and made a rash decision in 'becoming a Christian', so he frequents the old places, seeks out his old friends and indulges the old pleasures—all of which he temporarily left behind. Meeting with the church becomes a chore and a bore and is therefore minimized to once a Sunday, never mid-week.

The slow strangling process takes time, as I've said, and therefore he may keep up appearances for some considerable period. But his growing distaste for, and dissatisfaction with, the Bible, prayer, Christian fellowship and witnessing is matched by an escalating love for former things, the very life from which he had apparently escaped.

Those verses we quoted earlier from 2 Peter 2 also say that 'if they have escaped the corruption of the world by knowing our Lord and Saviour Jesus Christ and are again entangled in it and overcome, they are worse off at the end than they were at the beginning. It would have been better for them not to have known the way of righteousness, than to have known it and then to turn their backs on the sacred commandment that was passed on to them' (vv.20–21). Surely this is Peter's description of the thorny ground?

The picture that emerges is truly heartbreaking. Peter says it would be better for such people never to have known a thing about the Christian faith than to turn out as they do, flying in the face of all their privileges. They *knew* so much, they *experienced* a great deal, they had even *changed* quite dramatically for a while. But the important thing for us to realize is that they were *never really converted.*

As Peter says, 'Of them the proverbs are true: "A dog returns to its vomit," and, "A sow that is washed goes back to her wallowing in the mud"' (v.22). Their nature remains unchanged. Sin has not been rooted out. Radical rebirth just hasn't taken place, and so their reversion to type will happen sooner or later.

Dr Donald Grey Barnhouse tells how, when his European preaching tours took him to West Berlin, he would take the children to the world-famous zoo to see a huge sea-lion named Rupert. The animal weighed many hundredweight and they loved to watch him at feeding time when he would climb a platform and as the fish were thrown at him he'd lunge forward in an awesome dive, catch and swallow the fish in mid air and enter the pool with a massive explosion of water as his great bulk crashed through the surface.

Well, Dr Barnhouse filmed the action and later showed the film to his family. Sometimes, at the crucial point, he would switch the projector into reverse. Imagine the astonishing visual display as his viewers saw gallons of water arc in great plumes, as if from nowhere, into a mysterious hole in the surface, out of which emerged a huge sea-lion weighing between 3,000 and 4,000 pounds which then launched itself backwards on to a high platform while simultaneously spitting fish into a bucket!

What made all of this so incredibly amazing was that shown in reverse the whole action seemed both *impossible* and *grotesque.* But isn't this exactly what makes this apostasy we have been describing so terrifying and awesome? It seems *impossible* and *grotesque* for some to plunge, as it were, whole-heartedly into Christianity and later to withdraw from it totally, while at the same time belching forth with contempt and spitting out in derision that which they have learned of the Lord. But the parable of the sower assures us that this can happen, for this is the outcome for so many who hear the word. All this being so, how comforting it is that Jesus goes on to examine the factors which constitute true and lasting conversion.

The good soil—the valid conversion

> Still other seed fell on good soil, where it produced a crop—a hundred, sixty or thirty times what was sown... [this] is the man who hears the word and understands it. He produces a crop, yielding a hundred, sixty or thirty times what was sown (Mt 13:8, 23).

> But the seed on good soil stands for those with a noble and good heart, who hear the word, retain it, and by persevering produce a crop (Lk 8:15).

It is possible to tell by these words whether you or I are good soil or not. But this is not done by comparing yourself with other people. You may sit next to a 'hundred-fold' Christian and compare your 'thirty-fold' crop with his, with devastatingly discouraging results, decidedly *not* in your favour! This is to forget that God has different callings and vocations for each of his children and that 'when they measure themselves by themselves and compare themselves with themselves, they are not wise' (2 Cor 10:12).

What then are we to see in Jesus' words?

First, the word is received into a 'good and noble heart'. This means that the true convert possesses a heart which wants to hear *all* that God says and which doesn't balk or stumble at any aspect of divine truth. The privileges and responsibilities of commitment to Christ are understood, as is the fact that Jesus is both Saviour (to rescue us from the ruinous consequences of sin) and Lord (to direct our lives into the whole will of God). The love and justice of God are both understood and accepted equally, so that the appropriate responses are made from time to time in accordance with both aspects of God's being and nature.

Sin is viewed with revulsion and Christ is seen with an attraction that would forsake everything to follow him. The promise of heaven and the warnings of tribulation on earth are embraced with equal validity as the complete package for Christian disciples. The 'hard sayings' of Jesus won't cause them to stumble, for they came in with no preconceived conditions. There is total, unreserved commitment to all that Jesus said and all that he wishes for their lives.

Any 'convert' who can play fast and loose with the Bible ('yes, some of the things Jesus said *are* terrific, but those bits about hell, lakes of fire, outer darkness and stuff about him walking on water and being born of a virgin I just can't accept') is not 'good soil'. They have not got a noble heart. The mark of a true Christian is that he receives *all* that God said, simply because God said it. He'll suffer the stigma of being at odds with the moral climate of his age and the 'scientific' assertions of the intelligentsia where they conflict with the word of God. This is what it means to receive the word.

Secondly, he not only receives the word, he retains it. The element of *perseverance* must be there. Sun, wind, heat or cold cannot dislodge the seed from this heart. When many would-be disciples were deserting Jesus in large numbers, having taken offence at his teachings, Jesus asks the twelve, 'You do not want to leave too, do you?' to which Peter gives the memorable reply (the response of a 'retaining' heart): 'Lord, to whom shall we go? You have the words of eternal life. We believe and know that you are the Holy One of God' (Jn 6:67–68). No other options were open for Peter. His mind was made up. For good or ill, he was with Jesus.

To 'retain' is to hold fast, to cling on to something for all you're worth. For such a person unfaithfulness would be viewed as suicide. He is staking his life on this word and it is not a passing fad or occasional hobby. His whole eternal destiny is staked on the fact that what Jesus said must be true. Unlike false converts who draw the line and say, 'This far and no further,' true discipleship goes all the way. He would die rather than deny the Lord. The smile or disapproval of men, poverty or riches, trouble or ease are matters of comparative indifference to him, for he is set to follow the Lord. There can be no turning back.

Lastly, Jesus says that the true convert produces a crop. The good soil permits the seed of God's word to produce its full potential in the convert's life. He is totally responsive to the dynamic of God's word in its mind-changing and life-changing power. Its teachings, directives, principles and commands are all steadily and progressively implemented; family, friends, church life, work and leisure are all brought to the clear voice of God's word for counsel and direction. He lets God's word produce the fruit he wants to cultivate in his life. There are no blockages, arguments, rebellions or excuses.

Here, then, is that same true conversion we saw in the letter to the Hebrews: an illuminated mind, a persuaded heart convinced of all God says, and a responsive will which is ready to do all that God commands. All this combined with a clear public confession, proclaiming by lip and by life the designed fruits of the powerful word which God has sown into the good soil of a true heart.

Part Three:

Case Studies

7
David and Bathsheba—the Lure of Sexual Sin

In one of his books, Calvin Miller movingly describes a shocking event which happened just a few years ago. In the Vatican in Rome stands one of Michaelangelo's greatest works of art, the 'Pieta'. The artist has sculptured in stone the scene of Mary, the mother of the Lord, holding the limp and lifeless body of her Son after it had been removed from the cross. It is a marvellous expression of the artist's sensitivity and creativity, and has clearly been executed with deep feeling and emotion. It is, in short, a masterpiece. It has stood in its present location since 1499. Just a few years ago, a crazed assailant leapt the barrier which surrounded it and with a few well-placed hammer-blows, for ever defaced this work of creative genius. It is difficult to understand the attacker's aims or motivation, except to conclude that behind it lay some irrational, demonic desire to destroy that which is beautiful, wholesome and good.

Satan is just like this. He, too, wishes to vandalize and destroy every good work of God. He desires to smash it and twist it, to write his vile graffiti over the work of God's hands. Satan is out to break up good marriages, good homes and good lives.

That is why, with increasing frequency, we hear of

scandals involving the private lives of prominent Christian ministers or laymen. We have at times been stunned to hear of very gifted and perhaps internationally-known ministries suddenly being terminated because of the discovery of some sexual vice or extra-marital affair. A once fine reputation suddenly lies in tatters. A mighty flame for God is suddenly snuffed out. A once sharp and effective instrument in the Spirit's hands now lies blunted and rusting because it has been tainted by the corrosive acid of adultery.

The story of David and Bathsheba, recorded in 2 Samuel 11:1–12:25, stands as a startling and awesome example of the destructive power of sexual temptation and sin. 'It is a warning that a godly man can, in a moment of time, sully the achievements of a life time.'[8] Probably none of us feels immune from the temptation which assaulted David at this critical hour of his walk with God. Satan's intention to destroy the church means that individuals are often the focus of his unclean enticements, and sooner or later most of us will feel the pull of this enticing but deadly lure.

Sexual standards are swiftly eroded, not only in the world at large but also among God's professing people. In so many cases the world is already in the church. Christians seem to be losing their resistance to the pull of premarital and sometimes even extra-marital sex. It is common to hear, or to observe, instances of numerous flirtations, very 'physical' relationships among young single Christians, and even secret adulterous affairs, all of which are becoming commonplace in the church. One pastor from the West coast of America has written about the way in which sexual immorality has permeated the churches of the West.

> I do not think a week goes by but we hear of Christian leaders who have forsaken their wives, run off with the secretary, fallen into homosexuality or are facing some kind of moral crisis in their churches.

Satan seems to 'have a contract out' on marriages in general, and on Christian marriages in particular. He is bent on their destruction, primarily through the sexual unfaithfulness of one or both partners. His intention is to sap the spiritual strength of believers and of believing churches, and to erode their fortifications from within. The problem is not new. At the close of the Old Testament, Malachi exposed the spiritual ineffectiveness of his contemporaries. Among the many causes of this condition, which were specified by God's prophetic word, was this sin of adultery:

> The Lord is acting as the witness between you and the wife of your youth, because you have broken faith with her, though she is your partner, the wife of your marriage covenant.
>
> Has not the Lord made them one? In flesh and spirit they are his. And why one? Because he was seeking godly offspring. So guard yourself in your spirit, and do not break faith with the wife of your youth (Mal 2:14–15).

The enormity of this sin is brought home to us. God says, in effect, 'Do you see what you have done? She was yours from the beginning. You set your love on her in your youth. Your vows are as fresh in my sight today as the day you first exchanged them. Your partnership is irrevocable. Yours was a solemn commitment, and yet you are now so eager wilfully to vandalise your unity and to jeopardize the future of your seed—the children I have given to you!' The remedy? 'So guard yourself in your spirit, and do not break faith with the wife of your youth.' This is very much a 'battle for the mind', for it is there, it seems to me, where the battle is either lost or won.

As we turn to 2 Samuel 11, we notice that God permitted this powerful sexual temptation to come David's way, not in his youth, but in his middle age. A sexual temptation of great intensity assaulted his mind at a time when some of us might have concluded that he could easily handle it. This was not so. Perhaps it will never be so, even if we live to be a hundred! The time will come for each one of us (either sooner or later) when God will trust us with a trial in this area. God is testing whether you can be relied upon, and whether or not even greater avenues of service and usefulness should open up to you. God does not want you to fall, but rather to step higher. The tragedy here is that what could have been a 'stepping stone' to even greater ministry for David proved to be a 'stumbling block' issuing in an infamous fall of the first order, which rings down the centuries its funereal tones of frightening warning and ominous solemnity.

Little is said by most commentators about Bathsheba's part in all of this. I cannot prove this, but I believe that she deliberately planned the seduction of David in this way. Her approach seems to have been *premeditated.* It looks like she carefully anticipated the whole scenario well in advance. Certainly she offered no resistance to David's messengers and proposition to sleep with him (v.4). Maybe she was a bored housewife. Possibly she was ambitious. Whatever her motive, sexual sin always starts with what we dwell upon in our minds. As I said earlier, it is there that the battle is either lost or won. The likelihood is that Bathsheba lost the battle weeks or months before this fateful night.

Her approach was *explicit.* There was no subtlety here. If she did set out to seduce God's servant deliberately then she was far from subtle in her method of approach. She knew that the palace overlooked her penthouse suite. So why did she choose to bathe naked on the patio? She was absolutely shameless. She paraded her beauty and her nudity on the flat roof of her home in full view of the tall towers and ballustrades of the nearby palace. This may have been quite flattering to David, but it was to leave no question marks in his mind as to what she really intended. She was his for the asking.

Much seduction is, of course, more ambiguous and tentative than this. It is difficult to say which form is most powerful. The Bible condemns both approaches (Prov

7:17–18, 21–23). It is utterly wrong to try to awaken and arouse sexual desire in another person, *when those desires cannot righteously be satisfied.* It is wrong to light fires which cannot easily be extinguished and which will burn in the wrong place and cause devastating damage in the lives of all those who are touched by their illicit flames.

Christian girls need to be aware of the fact that men are aroused quickly by *what they see.* Jesus has forbidden fantasizing about sex with any other woman than one's wife (Mt 5:27–30). Christian girls can help the men to win that battle. The way they dress is important. Unclean thoughts need to be 'headed off at the pass', and so modest dress on the part of young ladies in our churches and conventions would be a great help.

Even so, we are warned here that it's likely that someone may set out quite deliberately to seduce us. American Christian leader, Larry Tomczak, describes what happened to a pastor friend of his acquaintance. The pastor was telephoned between 3 am and 4 am one night. His drowsy response to the phone was met by a tearful and distressed request for help from what sounded like a very desperate young lady in the fellowship. He told his wife and got dressed quickly in order to respond immediately to what sounded like a real emergency. Suddenly he felt a strong prompting from the Holy Spirit to call a male colleague, even at that unearthly hour. They would go and see the girl together. How much explanation his colleague needed I don't know, but they eventually arrived together at the door of the lady's third-floor flat. They rang her doorbell. When she answered the door, the girl stood in the hallway *totally naked.* Her intentions were obvious, but upon seeing the co-pastor standing there also, in total shock and surprise she slammed the door shut without letting either of the men in! Larry Tomczak relates how his pastor friend was honest enough to confide afterwards that at that early hour of the morning, when his defences were down, and this attractive woman made her approach in this explicit way, he didn't know what he would have done if the Holy Spirit had not provided the protection of a fellow minister to accompany him. We need to think about such pitfalls in advance, for many of us will meet *our* Bathsheba one day. The devil will see to that.

A number of factors made this temptation particularly alluring and irrefutable to David. It is instructive to consider some of these factors in order to learn from them.

(1) *It came at a high point in David's career.* David's long haul to the throne was over. Behind him lay a solid and consistent record of proven faithfulness and great victories. 2 Samuel 8 records how one enemy after another had fallen before him like skittles in a bowling alley in an unbroken run of resounding successes. He was popular with his people and had around him a team of faithful, gifted and reliable colleagues (2 Sam 8:15–18). He'd been able to lay some old scores to rest and had kept the promises he'd made to his late friend, Jonathan, way back in the difficult days which now lay behind him. The provision for Mephibosheth's restoration and royal pension served to demonstrate the security of David's position and the magnaminity of his heart (2 Sam 9). He could afford to relax. And even the recent trouble with the Ammonites (2 Sam 10) seemed no great worry to David. He felt he could delegate the handling of these troublemakers to trusted generals like Joab and Abishai. His personal presence would not be needed. He could stay at home.

And so, 'In the spring, at the time when kings go off to war . . . David remained in Jerusalem' (11:1). A terse and ominous statement which seems to prepare us for the tragedy which lay ahead.

Smugness, over-confidence, self-congratulation and idleness. These create a breeding ground for sudden and overwhelming temptation. When we've enjoyed success in public or private ministry, when we've received adulation, praise, 'big name' treatment, conference billing or popular authorship; when we are the focus of high expectations on the part of the people of God, it is at such times that we may lay ourselves wide open, in unguarded weakness, to the approach of powerful sexual temptation.

Men who continually run at full stretch are often peculiarly open to sensual diversions when they allow themselves time to relax or permit a brief vacation. Ministers, like bows, need unstringing at times. But they need to be careful that they do not slacken their guard. It is during these periods that they can often be found watching TV programmes or reading books and magazines which they shouldn't be looking at. We can tell ourselves: 'I'm entitled to some pleasure, some diversion. I've worked really hard lately . . .' And we can lull ourselves into a mood which is ready for Bathsheba. Let's beware of unstructured idleness, open-ended leisure and unguarded times of rest which may lay our lives unusually open to the devil's unclean suggestions as to how those periods may best be filled, which leads to our second observation about this temptation.

(2) *It was totally unexpected.* It came when all was going well for David and when he did not anticipate an approach like this from the wife of one of his commanders. He had little or no time to brace himself for the sudden assault upon his moral defences. He had no time to put on any special armour. He wasn't ready. It's not fair, but it's usually the case that the devil does not tap us on the shoulder and give advance warning of his strategy. Suddenly, there before us, is that powerful but unheralded temptation—in David's case it took the shapely form of Bathsheba.

Having said this, however, it is sometimes the case that sexual temptation makes its approaches much earlier and can be recognized for its devastating potential if we know what it is we're looking for. Dr Albert Mazat has suggested a number of danger signals by which we can put a check upon ourselves in this area. They include:

* Do I find myself drawn to a certain person to the extent that I look forward with unusual expectancy to planned meetings?
* Do I find myself making sure that I am particularly well groomed and well dressed at those times?
* What about my fantasies? Am I allowing myself to daydream, neglecting to put forbidden thoughts out of my head at once?
* Do I tell myself that the innuendoes and teasing that take place are just for fun, even though my pulse does sometimes race a bit?
* Do I encourage long looks, hesitations of glances, and sustained eye contact?
* What is my motive for a pat on the shoulder, a touch on the arm? Is it for the church member or is it for me?
* Am I guilty of small deceptions with my wife, not telling her of certain visits and phone calls?

These questions are helpful, for they assist us in the discovery of any weaknesses which may make us a prey to such unexpected temptations. This brings me to the third observation.

(3) *It was presented to a particular weakness in David's character.* The one area in David's life which he never seemed to have prayed about or deliberately subjected to the law of God was his love-life. A temptation is only a temptation if it has some attractiveness to us. David already had some seven wives and numerous concubines. We may conclude that he repeatedly gave in to his weakness and inability to control his sexual drive. When Bathsheba was seen bathing across the roof-tops of Jerusalem David might well have talked to himself in this way: 'If God meant me to say "no", then why did he let Bathsheba bathe on the roof just when I was suffering from insomnia and needed some air?' At those times Satan may whisper, 'You are special to God. He won't

mind. Others could not get away with this, but you can. God understands, he knows you can't help it. God knows that it's always been a problem for you. Go on, it's all right. God wouldn't have given you these feelings if he wanted you to suppress them. God will overlook it if it's just this once.'

And so the evil one draws us to perform that to which our minds and wills have already consented. John Hercus brings home the power of that moment:

> This was not suggestion, not fantasy. This was sheer seductive invitation. The most heady challenge in all David's life was there right in front of him, the richest prize in a life of conquest was there in all her naked loveliness only a stone's throw from his palace rooftop.[9]

This is how it is with sexual temptation—whether it is towards solo, pre-marital or extra-marital sex, it always comes with power and with very good reasons why a fall is unavoidable in our case. One of those reasons lies in our fourth observation.

(4) *It was very flattering.* I have alluded to this before. The peculiar factor in this is that the approach of middle age is usually the time when we begin to judge ourselves as least attractive to others. Most commentators are agreed that David was about fifty-one years of age at this point. A surprising number of men are susceptible to adultery at such a time. In his book, *Living at High Noon,* Gordon Macdonald seeks to explore the minds of such men in their 'mid-life crisis' and writes about a neighbour, Willard Solomon, presently trapped in the lure of an adulterous relationship:

> When Willard Solomon joins the young woman from the filing department at the restaurant, he is hard put to wonder why he waited so long to make such an encounter happen. What seems to have happened between them in a matter of minutes amazes him. A sudden strange sense of exhilaration rises within him, a seeming renewal of the 'mystery of the

> hunt' that he remembers well from his younger days. All his senses are at attention, each moment takes on significance. Why, he asks himself, is this so different from life at home with his wife?[10]

Macdonald then picks up on a suggestion first proposed by the Swiss psychiatrist, Carl Jung, that the human male tends to suppress the relational traits in his character in favour of the functioning or achieving drives. In his earlier years his self-worth is derived from his vocation, his career, his ambitions and his professional advancement. With the advent of middle age the picture becomes very different:

> But now things have changed; the career, once meteoric, is levelling off, and Willard Solomon finds himself a bit empty in spirit. Probe his thoughts, and you will discover that he feels cheated, but he doesn't know who did the cheating.[11]

This certainly applied to David. The record of his personal relationships is a very sad one indeed. The loner shepherd-boy, alienated from his father and his brothers from childhood onwards, never really seems to have found satisfaction in this department of his life and personality. His family life was a mess. His wife, Michal, never really understood him. Perhaps this pattern was repeated with his other six wives and numerous concubines. David surely longed for greater moments of intimacy and satisfaction in his personal relationships and for him, as for many like him, an adulterous affair holds promise of meeting those needs. If David's career had become somewhat boring, predictable and more than a little stagnant, Bathsheba offered the release of new thrills, new pleasures and new novelties. And so Gordon Macdonald sums up the peculiarly flattering excitement contained in this particular temptation in these words:

> In a world in which the slogan seems to be that 'everyone is doing it', it is not at all difficult for a bored man or woman to experiment with alternative relationships in which the 'electricity' will return.[12]

You may be middle-aged. You may judge yourself to be fat, faded and a failure, but you are probably handsome, attractive and charming in someone's eyes right through your whole lifetime. If, in addition, you are both rich and famous, then sooner or later someone will be asking for your number. Someone may want to make you feel young again, or at least provide you with the flattering opportunity for you yourself to try and prove that you still have what it takes.

Finally, we can add one last consideration with regard to David's temptation.

(5) *It was overwhelming in its forcefulness.* We are struck by the swiftness of David's response. He took no time to weigh this action or its possible consequences. In modern terms he was 'zapped', he 'fell in love' with the beautiful Bathsheba. If he had lived in the late twentieth-century Western world and not the Middle East of eleventh-century BC, he would have been heard muttering cliches like, 'This thing is bigger than both of us,' or, 'A man's gotta do what a man's gotta do,' or, 'We just couldn't help ourselves.' Either way, David entered unhesitatingly into what we moderns euphemize as a 'deep, meaningful relationship' with the unprotesting and very co-operative wife of Uriah the Hittite.

It is in this connection that we have to say that things are not likely to get any easier for Christians living in our contemporary world. The prevalence of pornography in all of its manifestations (films, magazines, novels, videos, comics and the suggestive humour of friends and workmates) will mean that sudden and often overwhelming attacks on our defences will confront most of us sooner or later, and probably on more than one occasion. The simple, and often not-so-subtle message in all of this is one which is saying, and saying insistently, 'If it feels good, do it . . . everybody else is.'

Powerful images tend to lodge in our minds and work away to erode the strength of our wills to the point where our, 'Well, I'm not so sure,' becomes a, 'So where's the harm really?' Eventually we find ourselves saying, 'OK, just this once, just for you.'

It is important to state here that I do not believe that sexual sin is to be equated with 'the unforgivable sin'. It is not. As soon as a person is converted, no matter how promiscuous their previous lifestyle has been, they are to know that they start afresh, clean in God's sight. The past really is forgiven, for 'the blood of Jesus... purifies us from every sin' (1 Jn 1:7). But the Lord comes to impart power to the lives of those he has made clean. What the Lord is interested in, when he has graciously wiped the slate of sexual sin clean in our lives, is that we then keep it clean.

If only David had stopped to think. It isn't enough at such times of powerful temptation to feel, 'I might be caught and found out' (David was). Nor even to be subdued by the thought, 'I could forfeit my future ministry' (to a certain extent David did). It isn't enough to realize that this act of passion may reap consequences, the like of which we may not, as yet, be fully aware. (Witness the subsequent affair with David's children Amnon and Tamar, and the career of his other sons Absalom and Adonijah.) No, what is needed is more than this. David must have been familiar with the story of how the power of God had operated in the life of Joseph who tackled a similarly unambiguous enticement to commit adultery in a wonderful and exemplary way.

If you turn to the record in Genesis 39:1–12, you will see how Joseph reacted when confronted with the unashamed sexual advances of Potiphar's wife.

(1) *Joseph reminded himself that someone trusted him*

> 'With me in charge,' he told her, 'my master does not concern himself with anything in the house; everything he owns he has entrusted to my care . . . My master has withheld nothing from me except you, because you are his wife' (vv.8–9).

Potiphar trusted Joseph. Potiphar knew that Joseph was God's man, and he therefore recognized his integrity and trusted him. Who trusted David? Surely many people did—his wives, his people, his army, his generals. Who trusts you? Any number of people, surely? It could be your parents who give you a measure of freedom to stay out late and go out with your girlfriend unchaperoned. It may be your marriage partner who understands the long hours you must work at the office each evening, or the trips you must take, or the ministry tours in which you're engaged, or the business dealings you must conduct in places far away. These are all part and parcel of God's call on your life. Are there people who look up to you as a model and exemplar of purity and power in the service of God? Then here is trust. Someone trusts you. Sexual sin is always a breach of somebody's trust. How can you betray that trust so honourably given?

(2) *Joseph was moved by a sense of love and loyalty to the one who would be hurt*

> My master has withheld nothing from me except you, because you are his wife (v.9).

She was Potiphar's life partner, his possession, his property, his wife. Joseph had a very high view of marriage, even if it was a 'pagan' marriage. This woman was not, nor ever could be, Joseph's. Similarly, David ought to have realized that Bathsheba's body belonged to someone else—to the Lord in the first instance, and in a very real sense to her husband also (see 1 Corinthians 7:4). She could never legitimately belong to David. Yet David never considered for a moment the violation of solemn boundaries entailed in his wilful act of adultery. He never weighed, even for a second, the misery his lust would bring to the heart of Uriah (should he find out), to Bathsheba (should her sin be uncovered) or to himself (should God fail to overlook the seriousness of this act). It was *theft*.

How wise of the prophet Nathan to major on this solemn aspect of David's sin when, some months later, as he spoke to the unrepentant king, Nathan metaphorically 'pinned' David to his throne with the nails of conviction as he told the piercing parable of the rich herdsman who stole his poor neighbour's only ewe lamb (2 Sam 12). The essence of David's sin was that he had cruelly stolen that which belonged to another. It was this consideration which weighed so heavily with Joseph and enabled him to stand strong when temptation came with power.

(3) *Joseph was acutely conscious of his standing before God*

> How then could I do such a wicked thing and sin against God? (v.9).

It was not fear of detection, fear of conception or fear of infection which stopped Joseph—it was fear of God.

Unlike David, whose eyes were temporarily blinded by the blazing fires of his own lust, Joseph could still be shocked by sin. God doesn't call sex outside of marriage 'doing what comes naturally', he calls it *'wicked'*, and so should you and I. It was C. S. Lewis who pointed out that 'the monstrosity of sexual intercourse outside of marriage is that those who indulge in it are trying to isolate one kind of union (the sexual) from all other kinds of unions which were intended to go along with it and make up the total union'. And in the same vein, David Prior, when commentating on 1 Corinthians 6:15–16 and the almost totally amoral situation which prevailed in first-century Corinth said:

> Why is pre-marital intercourse wrong? Why are homosexual practices wrong? Why is adultery wrong? Simply because there is no true oneness and therefore there is no one-flesh either ... the problem here was intimacy without intention, communion without commitment.[13]

But to read 2 Samuel 11 is to conclude that David, if he

even thought of God at all, must have imagined that God had grown old and senile. It's as though, to David, God was deaf, blind and the helpless victim of a failing and fading memory. Did he imagine that God couldn't see all of this? If we would be kept from falling into sexual sin, then we must be marked deep within by a proper love of and respect for God. Is God alive to you in your experience?

Is he moving, motivating and empowering you to keep clean? For if you are good looking, attractive and desirable, and if at the same time you are feeling bored, lonely and unloved, then only one thing will keep you from sexual sin when its temptation comes with overwhelming power: the fear of God.

(4) *Joseph was prepared to take prompt, even drastic action*

As the wife of Potiphar became more and more insistent with her approaches, we notice that Joseph at first said 'No'. His mind would not consent to do what his spirit told him was wrong. He utterly refused to be drawn into the whirlpool of illicit sex, either mentally or physically. He refused even to be with the woman. He avoided her company, making contact only when it was absolutely necessary to the performance of his duties (v.10).

But the temptress did not give up, 'she spoke to Joseph day after day' (v.10) and later 'caught him by his cloak and said, "Come to bed with me"' (v.12). Joseph only had one option left. He *ran!* 'But he left his cloak in her hand and ran out of the house' (v.12b). Not very macho! A blow to his own self-esteem, perhaps, to be seen involved in the indignity and humiliation of actually *running* from a situation he knew he couldn't handle. But isn't this what David should have done? He could have run, he could have averted his eyes; he could have drawn the drapes; he could have summoned a battle conference; he could have ridden out of Jerusalem and joined his generals in the war with the Ammonites. There are any number of things he could have done to flee this temptation.

Canadian author and Christian psychiatrist, John White, honestly admits the weaknesses most men are prey to: 'I find that my own eyes like to stray where my conscience tells me not to, and that my juices are on the side of my eyes rather than on the side of my conscience.' He then goes on to ask, 'Am I a freak? Am I a dirty old man?' but answers with words of encouragement and resolve:

> Well I suppose I could be both if I let myself be. But at the point where I am (pleasurably) jolted by the magazine rack as I buy a newspaper, I am still a free being. God has set me free. I therefore, like Job, have made a covenant with my eyes not to look where they should not look, and with my mind not to play games with what I inadvertently (or deliberately) saw.[14]

In the event, of course, David did none of these things. And so with something akin to a dry mouth, a beating heart and a choking lump of emotion in our throats, we must follow through the momentous aftermath of these events.

David sent Bathsheba back home. The whole evening might well have been forgotten, or it could have become the first of many clandestine 'arrangements' between the palace and the home of one of the King's subjects, a long-run and torrid extra-marital affair, about which Uriah would know nothing. Might have been, but for one thing—Bathsheba became pregnant. Had this happened in our generation the first answer to suggest itself would have been simple: murder the baby. But the obscenity of abortion was not readily available. Yet David's heart did walk down that road of guilt, shame and deceit to the point where he, too, seriously contemplated murder. Not the murder of the baby, but the murder of Bathsheba's husband.

In the total integrity with which the Bible describes the failings of so many of its 'heroes', the grim aftermath is unfolded in considerable detail. How true to life and human nature it all is. We squirm at David's awkward and unsuccessful attempts at a cover-up, a cover-up which was foiled at every turn due to Uriah's keen sense of loyalty to David and to his fellow troops still at war in the field. Uriah could see no justification for allowing himself the luxury and diversion of a night with his wife while his men still bore the heat of battle.

We are then caused to gasp in sheer horror and unbelief as the 'sweet psalmist of Israel' treacherously despatches his trusting officer back to the front line bearing sealed orders which amount to no more than a death warrant—Uriah is to be positioned in such jeopardy by Joab, the commanding officer, that his death is almost a guaranteed result: 'Put Uriah in the front line where the fighting is fiercest. Then withdraw from him so that he will be struck down and die' (2 Sam 11:15).

Adultery. Lying. Deceit. Murder. A catalogue of sins which were to plunge David into one of the darkest periods of his life, spiritually speaking. Authorities differ as to how much time lapsed before God sent the prophet Nathan to expose the situation. It appears that David remained in this unrepentant condition for between twelve and eighteen months. That is a long time. A *very* long time when we recall David's own retrospect upon his feelings as he has recorded them in Psalm 32 and Psalm 51.

These psalms vividly capture David's moods of misery and guilt during what Tom Houston calls the period of 'his deepest fall and perhaps his sublimest recovery'.[15] David 'kept silent' throughout this whole time (Ps 32:3), refusing to confess his sin either to God or to man. There is no doubt, however, that his conscience continually voiced its accusations in his ear. David records all of the psychosomatic effects induced by a troubled and violated conscience—the weariness, sleep loss, depression of appetite and so on (Ps 32:3–4). This went on until the point was reached where David's heart was broken and he could truly admit 'I have sinned against the Lord' (2 Sam 12:13).

David had backslidden very badly indeed. What is more, he had backslidden for a very long time. Yet God restored him.

God wants to restore all backsliders. The human instrument which God used in David's restoration was a faithful man speaking faithful words even at great personal risk to himself. In Nathan, the prophet, we see a man moving obediently under divine prompting and delivering with accurate and unmistakable pointedness all that God wanted spoken into that situation. If Nathan had been tempted to fudge the issue and to blunt the edge of his verbal sword, then there is no indication whatsoever that he yielded to that particular temptation even for a moment.

Although at first David did not see himself in the parable, and did not know that the judgement he had pronounced was upon himself (2 Sam 12:5–6), Nathan left no room for escape. 'You are the man!' thundered the prophet, as the sharp two-edged sword of Christ's word was plunged *mercifully* into David's heart. Nathan was the best friend David had. Nathan told David explicitly what conscience had only been able to mumble through the layers of suppression which David had applied to his heart and mind for the last year or so. Nathan's faithful wounding of his friend is recorded for us:

> This is what the Lord, the God of Israel says: 'I have anointed you king over Israel, and I delivered you from the hand of Saul. I gave your master's house to you, and your master's wives into your arms. I gave you the house of Israel and Judah. And if all this had been too little, I would have given you even more. Why did you despise the word of the Lord by doing what is evil in his eyes?' (2 Sam 12:7–9).

Sin can be forgiven, and yet we may live with the consequences of that sin. It is the working out of the principle announced in Galatians 6:7–8, 'Do not be deceived: God cannot be mocked. A man reaps what he sows.' A man who punches his hand through a plate glass window in a drunken fit, thus slashing his arm, may subsequently be converted and dramatically changed. The scars, however, will remain. It is true that God forgave David, but Uriah was to remain dead, and God's chastening hand was still to fall on the couple. The baby conceived in their adultery was taken away from them (2 Sam 12:14).

There was to be even greater severity than this. God told him that he would suffer the shame of public exposure (2 Sam 12:12) and that the ripples of evil influence would move in ever-widening circles throughout his family (vv.10–11). The consequences of sin for a spiritual and political leader may be far greater than those experienced by the average man whose calling places him less prominently in the public eye (cf. 1 Tim 5:19–20; Jas 3:1). The greater our privilege, the greater our responsibility, and the more accountable we are for sin and waywardness in the pursuit of that privileged calling.

The backslider is the most miserable man or woman on earth. The sooner such a one takes words of sincere sorrow and repentance and returns to the Lord, the better. God wants to heal the broken spirit of the backslider and cause him to rejoice again.

If this chapter has spoken personally to you, what better words could you take with you on your return to the Lord than the words first spoken by David in Psalm 51.

It could be that it's been a long time since you've opened a Bible. Why not turn to Psalm 51? It would be a great place to start.

8

Peter—the Slippery Slope of Backsliding

As we turn to some solemn words of Jesus, predicting the inevitability of a sad lapse in the lives of his disciples, we are struck by the note of realism they sound in our understanding of the Christian life. Reared in what someone has called 'the thumbsucking generation', we have grown used to a soft, cushioned existence in which the ideal envisaged is one of cradle-to-grave security. We expect a smooth ride wherever we go. We view the Christian pathway as consisting of all frills and thrills with no spills; and that conversion ought to introduce us to a life which amounts to no less than one long summer vacation with no autumn or winter to intrude upon us and break up our bliss.

But facing his own dark hour with the enemy, Jesus knew that his disciples would pass through distressing trials simply because of their connection with him. As he took them across the Kedron valley to the place of his own arrest in Gethsemane, he warned them in these solemn words recorded in Mark 14:27–31:

> 'You will all fall away,' Jesus told them, 'for it is written: "I will strike the shepherd, and the sheep will be scattered." But after I have risen, I will go ahead of you into Galilee.'
>
> Peter declared, 'Even if all fall away, I will not.'

> 'I tell you the truth,' Jesus answered, 'today—yes, tonight—before the cock crows twice you yourself will disown me three times.'
>
> But Peter insisted emphatically, 'Even if I have to die with you, I will never disown you.' And all the others said the same.

We are going to focus upon Peter's shameful denial of the Lord. But what Jesus said here he said to them all. What happened to Peter could happen to any one of us. Judas had already left to carry out the dirty business of betrayal as he played the part of a lackey to the authorities. What Jesus now says is meant for all of *us,* even if we could never envisage ourselves playing the part of a Judas. Backsliding is an ever-present threat to the unconscientious believer. What, according to Jesus, precipitates its occurrence?

Jesus highlights the dangers

1. Ignoring Scripture predictions of trouble in the Christian life (v.27)

Jesus quotes an ancient prophecy from Zechariah 13:7, 'I will strike the shepherd and the sheep will be scattered.' In this prediction of Jesus' sufferings the disciples are to see the hand of God behind all that buffeted their Master. The Father's hand would strike Jesus in such a way as to amaze, astonish and appal the disciples. It would create in them so much fear that they would run in panic.

The Scriptures promise us trouble because of our connection with Jesus: 'In this world you will have trouble' (Jn 16:33). 'We must go through many hardships to enter the Kingdom of God' (Acts 14:22). 'Do not be surprised at the painful trial you are suffering, as though something strange were happening to you' (1 Pet 4:12). If we don't know this or don't believe it, then that trouble, when it comes, will be a major cause of stumbling to us. Such warnings cannot be 'tippexed' out of Scripture. They are an inevitable accompaniment to the Christian life.

2. Deprivation of leadership in time of crisis (v.27b)

If the leader is removed, those he leads will be scattered. Historically, persecution has always aimed at the arrest, imprisonment and removal of church leaders as a top priority. The leaders are the first to die. Jesus says in effect, 'Without my presence it will be well nigh impossible for you to stand.' This being so, how foolish is the thinking of those nomadic, drifting, 'tumbleweed' Christians who wilfully refuse to receive protection and input from Christian leaders in the life of a local church. They are totally unprepared for trouble, since trouble was never meant to be faced alone. We all need the security of strong fellowship and faithful leadership if we are to face crises with some hope of victory.

3. Facing sudden shock and being totally unprepared (v.27a)

The word translated 'you will all *fall away*' is related to our English word 'scandalized' and meant in the original 'you will be like animals caught in a trap'. That's the nature of many occasions of discouragement. They enfold us with the suddenness and surprise of the jaws of a trap snapping tight around the limbs of its unwary victim.

How many Christians start their road to backsliding because they see things which shock and scandalize them? For the Twelve it would be the sight of Jesus arrested, buffeted, beaten and crucified. For us it may be the collapse of a respected church leader or some scandal which sweeps the church. Such events expose the depth of our understanding of God's word and the level of our trust in the Lord. If we lean on men, they will disappoint us. 'The best of men are men at best.' We all need human leadership, as I have just said, but ultimately our real security must lie much deeper than that—it must be in the

Lord himself.

4. Being oblivious to the schemes of the devil

The parallel passage in Luke contains these words, 'Simon, Simon, Satan has asked to sift you as wheat.' This indicates that in many of the pressures we face which cause us to backslide, Satan has sought God's permission to get involved and that permission has been granted. The grain of your Christian profession is being threshed violently. Satan wants to see us fall, and fall badly. He lusts after our ruin in order to cast this back into the face of God and so, inevitably, we become the focus of his hatred against God. Satan wants to rid us of wheat and leave only chaff, but be encouraged! The reason God gave him permission to try us is that God wants to rid us of chaff and leave only wheat. The devil is never allowed to thresh us more violently than the degree to which God allows him to move, and which is also never beyond that with which we can cope (1 Cor 10:13). Satan is only given so much rope—he cannot exceed the restraints of God's permission in pressurizing our lives.

5. Not listening well to the words of Jesus

The utterly unprepared state of the disciples when Jesus the Shepherd was struck was due to their dullness in hearing Jesus' predictions of those terrible events. On at least two previous occasions Jesus had predicted his death in some detail (Mk 8:31; 10:33). He was preparing them for the tough time which lay ahead but, like so many disciples today, they just weren't listening. The sixteenth-century English Reformer, Bishop Hugh Latimer, tells in one of his sermons of a poor lady who suffered from insomnia. All the sleeping draughts and potions supplied by her physicians had failed to induce the precious sleep she needed. Her own brainwave suggestion was to take her to the local parish church for she reasoned, 'I have slept soundly there every Sunday morning for years!' Like a lot of Christians she slept soundly at the very time she should have been awake. The word we have not heard will not be there to help us when we need it most.

6. Comparing ourselves with others and coming out tops (v.29)

Peter's self-confidence emerges clearly: 'Even if all fall away, I will not.' He looks at the other ten men and doesn't deny the truth of what Jesus said about *them* falling away. He's just sure that he personally will be the *one* exception. How easy it is to imagine that the sins which have trapped others—materialism, sexual immorality, drunkenness or fear—could never get a hold on us. It is the person who thinks he stands who is in most need to be on guard, said the Apostle Paul, lest he fall (1 Cor 10:12).

7. Bulldozing our way through sober warnings (vv.30–31)

Jesus went on to predict that within hours, even before daybreak, Peter would have denied all knowledge of Jesus not once only but no less than *three* times! His cocksure reply—'Even if I have to die with you, I will never disown you'— is not just just further evidence of his misplaced self-confidence, it constitutes a dangerous stubbornness which would dare even to contradict the words of Jesus himself. He reminds us of those Christians who hastily conclude, 'Well I could never fall for *that* temptation again,' or, 'How could she have done such a thing? I could never allow such a weakness to enter into *my* life.' The examples of tragic falls in Scripture and also in our personal acquaintance seem to leave such people without a flicker of fear that the same lapse could happen to them. And yet before breakfast television goes on the air tomorrow you could have fallen into a treacherous denial of Jesus, gross immorality or an abdication from your responsibilities of the very worst kind. You don't think so? That's exactly what Peter and all the others said, and they were wrong too.

So now, as we turn to the account of what actually happened to Peter, we must take warning not only from the precipitating causes of his fall just listed, but also from its actual ingredients. For our purposes, what is so disturbing about the backslider is that, poised as he is between belief and unbelief, we are in no place to say whether he is a true Christian or not from any outward appearances. The no-man's land he's chosen to inhabit makes the direction of his life hard to predict. Will he be restored or will he prove to be a complete apostate? The fact that the answer to these questions remains unclear to others and often to himself, should be the greatest incentive for all of us to take warning from Peter, and shun this condition for the dangerous quicksands it represents.

Tradition tells us that Mark recorded his gospel from the personal memoirs of Peter himself. If this is true, then Peter told Mark about his failures in open integrity and honesty in order to benefit generations of believers for all time. We need to listen to one who tasted the bitterness of backsliding so that we won't feel drawn to experiment with its poisoned waters for ourselves.

Backsliding begins, as we've seen, in the indulgence of a proud unteachable spirit which refuses to take Jesus' warnings as in any way relevant to one's own life. That's surely why Peter and the rest slept in Gethsemane. Who needs to pray against temptation if one already walks in immunity from it (Mk 14:38)? So the temptation, when it came, took them all by surprise, including the presumptuous hero, Peter. After an aborted attempt to save Jesus and a reckless display of violence in cutting off the servant's ear, Peter joined in the panic of the others and fled.

Peter is now following Jesus at a distance (Mk 14:54). Reckless courage has yielded to cowardice. To stay close to Jesus would involve him in personal danger, verbal abuse, criticism and pain. The backslider fears following the Lord fully. Other voices whisper, 'Don't be fanatical! Don't take this too seriously!' Church involvement becomes spasmodic and casual. The Bible is rarely opened. Prayer becomes a neglected practice.

But nature abhors a vacuum. Other things rush in to replace the emptiness experienced during this cooled relationship with the Lord.

And so, like Peter, the backslider may drift into bad company. 'Peter followed Jesus at a distance, right into the courtyard of the high priest. There he sat with the guards and warmed himself at the fire' (v.54). Psalm 1:1 warns us not to 'walk in the counsel of the wicked . . . stand in the way of sinners . . . or sit in the seat of mockers.' The Apostle Paul said, 'Bad company corrupts good character' (1 Cor 15:33).

Of course, a believer may find himself in dubious company in order to try and win those people for the Lord. But that's not why Peter was there. Bad company is always dangerous, but never more dangerous than when we're in it for the wrong reasons. With Peter it was 'to warm himself by the fire'. The backslider always chooses such company in order to *take* from and not *give* to them. He 'warms himself by the fire' of their friendships (perhaps the excitement of a sexual relationship), or their entertainments (seeking diversion in twisted books or films), or their intellectual stimulus (debating with cynical sceptics who mount the big-guns of their arguments against the Bible and the Christian faith). Some take 'A' levels or degrees which they know will seriously erode their confidence in the Bible as the word of God.

Others warm themselves at the fire of false religious devotion in a church which denies the cross and the deity of Christ, and preaches only an emaciated caricature of Christianity. Still others work their way into the 'in-crowd' of a circle of blasphemous and totally promiscuous workmates. Matthew Henry said that 'those who warm themselves with evil-doers grow cold towards good people and good things'.

Please understand that I'm not advocating a false type of Christian monasticism as an alternative to this. The answer is not in seeking out a Christian enclave or ghetto of pious believers hermetically sealed from the corrupting influence of the world. In all this the question becomes, 'Who is most influencing whom?' And the answer to that question is the deciding factor in determining whether or not the company we keep is good for us.

Another tell-tale sign of a backslider in trouble is when, like Peter, *he's seeking to keep his discipleship a well-hidden secret.* While Peter was below in the courtyard one of the servant girls of the high priest came by. When she saw Peter warming himself she looked closely at him. 'You also were with that Nazarene, Jesus,' she said. But he denied it: 'I don't know or understand what you're talking about' (Mk 14:66–68). Far from confessing Christ before men, the backslider is unlikely to be telling anyone that he is a Christian. He may have postponed indefinitely the initial New Testament way of doing this—being baptized (Mk 16:15–16; Acts 2:41–42). He wishes that the Christian faith resembled that of the Freemasons—a secret affair in which one's true identity is known only to those in the faith themselves. But it isn't like that in authentic Christianity. We have to go public, and sooner rather than later.

When Jesus-stickers were something of a craze among Christians, I recall travelling on a train wearing a purple and day-glo orange sticker on my lapel, bearing the slogan 'Jesus is Lord'. One passenger opposite me was boring a hole in my chest as he gazed at this badge. It's moments like that when you wonder if it wouldn't have been wiser to remain anonymous, and to keep your discipleship a closely-guarded secret.

There's an ever-present pressure to deny Jesus in word or in action. But if you are presently papering over your profession of faith in an attempt to disguise the fact that you're a Christian, then that's the mark of a backslider.

And of course such denials escalate: 'Again he denied it... he began to call down curses on himself, and he swore to them, "I don't know this man you're talking about"' (vv.69–71). What was in fact no big test at first (a servant girl), grew in pressure. One girl became many men as the soldiers round the fire joined in too. And what began as uneasy and ambiguous evasion became strong denial under oath, even with bitterness and cursing.

People may say, 'You don't go to church and read the Bible, do you?' as if the whole idea certified us as the possessors of only half a brain; mere mindless morons. A nervous reply like Peter's, 'I can't think what you mean!' may soon necessitate other lies to cover up totally our connection with Christ—even to the point where the old 'fisherman's language' surfaces once again (v.71). Peter is seeking the approval of men, not the commendation of Jesus. Yet, even here, it's good to see that Peter cursed *himself* and not Jesus (v.71). There are some sins even a backslider cannot commit. Cursing Jesus is one of them (1 Cor 12:3). But what a fall! Peter is here anathematizing himself, giving himself over to destruction, to unimaginable harm if his denial of knowing Jesus didn't prove true. You and I could fall a long way once we're on the slippery slope of backsliding, and who's to say where it all could end?

The point of all this is that the logical conclusion of that slippery slope is total apostasy from the faith. So who wants to embark voluntarily on that dangerous course? Surely none of us. Two things kept Peter from falling completely, and I wish to draw your attention to them at this point as they will greatly encourage us too.

1. The 'seed of God' within him

'No-one who is born of God will continue to sin, because God's seed remains in him; he cannot go on sinning, because he has been born of God' (1 Jn 3:9). 'We know that anyone born of God does not continue to sin; the one who was born of God keeps him safe, and the evil one does not touch him' (1 Jn 5:18).

Just as a magnetic needle will always revert to pointing due north, so a believer, no matter how far he's turned from the Lord, will always return. He cannot be de-magnetized or repolarized! An irreversible change has taken place within him. It goes against the *pull* of his inner man for him to turn away from the Lord and to embark upon a course of backsliding.

To change the simile, an underground spring may become blocked to such a degree with soil and debris that it apparently dries up the invisible source of water running below. But such is the inward pressure of that stream, that before long the spring will eventually gush forth once again with renewed vigour. Such is the life within God's children. Peter had it. Judas didn't. That is sufficient reason to explain the difference between these two men. But there's more here to explain the eventual restoration of Peter.

2. The prayer of Jesus for him

'But I have prayed for you, Simon, that your faith may not fail' (Lk 22:32). This is the pattern of Jesus' intercession, which he continues now in heaven, for all true believers.

It is repeated again in John 17:11–15 'Holy Father, protect them by the power of your name . . . none has been lost except the one doomed to destruction [Judas] . . . protect them from the evil one.' Paul glories in it in Romans 8:34, 'Christ Jesus . . . is at the right hand of God and is also interceding for us,' and so does the writer to the Hebrews: 'He is able to save completely those who come to God through him, because he always lives to intercede for them' (Heb 7:25). Jesus prays that the faith of true believers will never *completely* collapse. His prayers are always answered!

This then is the two-fold guarantee that we shall come back to the Lord just as Peter did. And it is moving to see exactly how this return began, for the power of this new life and of Jesus' intercession goes to work even at the point where Peter has sunk to his lowest ebb. But before we see that, perhaps a word or two more on our guaranteed security as believers would be in order. Because, of course, many other factors within Scripture bear upon the ultimate safety of men and women like Peter who, buffeted by Satan, may feel a very real hesitation to conclude they could never ultimately be lost or prove to be apostate.

For Peter (or any of us who truly believe in Jesus) to be lost, certain impossible things must happen. Not only, as we have seen, must the seed of life which God has planted within us become utterly extinguished and snuffed out; and in addition the powerful prayers of Jesus Christ be silenced and his presence removed from the throne of intercession, but also a whole list of sheer *impossibilities* must take place as well.

God must be persuaded that he made the wrong choice in electing us and loving us in the first place, a love that was set upon us before time. Ephesians 1:4 says, 'For he chose us in him before the creation of the world to be holy and blameless in his sight. In love he predestined us to be adopted as his sons through Jesus Christ, in accordance with his pleasure and will.' Since he did not choose us because of any foreseen good within us, but rather *in spite of* our ruin in sin, then no lapse, no matter how terrible (short of complete apostasy), can thwart the course of God's predestination or repulse the persistence of his love.

Is it possible that some new unforeseen defilement or ugliness could enter into our minds or our lives which could then blot out our fitness to stand in God's presence or be the recipients of his love? Of course not. Didn't Paul ask, 'Who shall separate us from the love of Christ?' (Rom 8:35) and conclude emphatically that *nothing* could do so (Rom 8:38–39)?

Furthermore, the Bible tells us that the names of the redeemed are written in the 'Lamb's book of life' (see Revelation 20:15; 21:27 and compare Daniel 12:1; Luke 10:20). Is it possible that there is an eraser big enough to penetrate the closely-guarded fortresses of heaven and blot out for ever the name of even one person written there? Surely not. The whole idea is preposterous.

Furthermore, could Jesus' death prove defective at any point—strong enough to convert and save in its effectual power, but not strong enough to keep those whom it has washed, justified and saved? The Apostle Paul believed it couldn't:

> He who did not spare his own Son, but gave him up for us all—how will he not also, along with him, graciously give us all things? Who will bring any charge against those whom God has chosen? It is God who justifies. Who is he that condemns? Christ Jesus, who died—more than that, who was raised to life—is at the right hand of God and is also interceding for us. Who shall separate us from the love of Christ? (Rom 8:32–35).

The death of Christ has power to keep to the end, as well as to save at the beginning.

The last impossibility I will mention is that of the Holy Spirit being persuaded to vacate and abandon the hearts of those he has once consented to indwell. This is a desertion which could never happen since 'having believed, you were marked in him with a seal, the promised Holy Spirit, who is a deposit guaranteeing our inheritance until the redemption of those who are God's possession—to the praise of his glory' (Eph 1:13–14).

It is all of these factors and more which unite their force even in the hearts of grossly backslidden believers and trigger or set in motion the processes by which their return and restoration are guaranteed. How did this happen with Peter?

At the moment of his third, most vehement denial, circumstances began to trigger his seared conscience into action. The cock crowed (Mk 14:72). An everyday, almost incidental, occurrence for most people in Jerusalem at that time. But not for Peter. In Peter's case it was a reminder from God of who he really was. God may bring old Christian friends your way, or cause you to step into a very significant meeting at church, or hear a message just for you, or read a magazine in the dentist's waiting-room, or receive a letter that comes from an old acquaintance telling you she's become a Christian. God can make the cock crow loud and clear in your ears, announcing the painful reminder of what Jesus said to you and of who you really are.

As with Peter who 'remembered the word Jesus had spoken to him', the triggering circumstances of your own personal 'cock crow' may bring back a host of memories and truths which flood the mind, storm the defences, and melt that hardened heart. Luke tells us (Lk 22:61) that it was at this precise moment that Peter saw Jesus' face in the house of the high priest and those tender, pitying eyes of welcoming love, with which Jesus stared at Peter, were to complete the timely ministry of that noisy crow. Peter broke down and wept bitterly. The backslider had begun to repent. The backslider was returning. They always do eventually.

Imagine yourself lost one stormy night on some God-forsaken moorland, perhaps in the Yorkshire Dales or the deserted moors of Devon. The rain is lashing your face. The wind bites through every fold of your paltry clothing. Your fingers are stiffening and blue with the cold. Your mood is one of near despair. Suddenly and miraculously, as if from nowhere, a bus appears, its lights piercing the darkness, its friendly red paintwork giving way to a warm, well-lit interior filled with the faces of snug, unworried people who, far from being lost, are heading home to their families and friends. The bus stops to rescue you, the astonished stranger. At that point you have two choices. You can stay out in the rain and the cold and quite probably die. Or you can board the bus and let it speed you home to safety and security. The choice is yours.

The first choice is the foolish and almost unbelievable option taken by the apostate. The second is the one that is presented to the backslider sooner or later. The backslider must come in out of the cold. To do so is both his nature and his destiny.

Ask Peter, he should know.

9

Gehazi—Don't Miss Your Destiny

In Charles Dickens' classic tale *A Christmas Carol,* the old miser Ebenezer Scrooge passes through one of the most traumatic nights possible when on Christmas Eve he is visited by the ghost of his old business partner, Marley, and also by the spirits of Christmas past, Christmas present and Christmas future. The spirit of Christmas future opens up Ebenezer's eyes to see the grim spectacle of a rapidly approaching death which snatches Scrooge away, utterly friendless, deserted and alone, and brings home to his conscience the agonizing retrospect of a totally wasted life and the unenviable prospect of an unwanted and unmissed departure from this world.

The Bible is full of the equally frightening scenes of those who have begun well and ended tragically, wasting their lives, forfeiting their ministries, and missing their destiny. Often such great losses turn around a crucial series of events or choices which actually put before us momentous decisions and commitments to be made. If we make the wrong decision we can bring into our lives the most serious of consequences. The questions then become: 'Could you miss out on God's best for your life? Could you fall short of all that God has intended for you?'

Scripture answers that question unequivocally: '*Yes you*

could.' When we remember how Esau sold his birthright, Lot chose Sodom, Moses forfeited the promised land, Samson fell into enemy hands as a man both blinded and enslaved, Saul lost his kingship and Solomon decayed into debauchery, disappointment and emptiness, we realize that examples are virtually piled up to warn us of the possibilities. In the pages of the New Testament also, we see how Ananias and Sapphira lied to the Holy Spirit with the most dire consequences, and how Demas forsook the Apostle Paul because he 'loved this world' (2 Tim 4:10). Jesus spoke of the 'wicked lazy servant' who buried the money entrusted to him and had nothing to show for his life's work when the Master came to call his servants to account (Mt 25:14–30).

One of the Apostle Paul's greatest fears was that he would one day prove to be a reject. He says in 1 Corinthians 9:26–27,

> Therefore I do not run like a man running aimlessly; I do not fight like a man beating the air. No, I beat my body and make it my slave so that after I have preached to others, I myself will not be disqualified for the prize.

The phrase 'disqualified for the prize' actually translates only one word in the original, *adokimos,* a word which is variously rendered 'disqualified', 'disapproved', 'rejected' or 'castaway'. It has led some to postulate that what Paul here feared was the possibility of losing his own salvation. The man who wrote the magnificent eighth chapter of Romans could hardly have stood in fear of that! No, what concerned the Apostle, as is obvious from the context, was something quite different. He has spoken at length about his ministry as an apostle (1 Cor 9:1) and how this ministry was thrust upon him as an offer he couldn't refuse, presumably when the Lord Jesus apprehended him on the road to Damascus. The chapter speaks of the tremendous application and single-mindedness with which Paul gave himself to that ministry (vv.19–25), and that what most concerned him was that he could behave like an unfit, lazy or compromised athlete who had somehow been disqualified from the race and had forfeited the winner's prize. In other words, he feared losing his ministry and its reward on the Day of Judgement.

Many a Christian has forfeited his calling in the Lord's service through a moral lapse, serious doctrinal deviation, or unwise entanglement with others in his personal relationships. What Paul feared, then, was the possibility of the Lord 'shelving' his ministry because he, Paul, was no longer fit enough morally and spiritually to perform it. He was afraid of rejection, of proving so derelict in his duties that the Lord was left with no choice other than to insist upon early retirement and in effect cause Paul to be made redundant, as far as his Christian ministry was concerned, for the rest of his life.

One of the most instructive examples in Scripture of how such a thing can happen is the history of Elisha's personal associate, Gehazi. His sad decline shows us that testings of our true calibre often turn around a series of crucial events and happenings, the real significance of which we are usually blind to at the time. It seems to me that the days in which we presently live cause God's people to face similar sifting challenges. Gone are the days when we could 'play church' for years and simply treat our Christian lives as an absorbing hobby or occasional pastime.

The forces of darkness, and the moving of God's Spirit, seem to be gathering such momentum around us that it appears to me that things will never again 'tick over nicely, thank you very much' in our churches. A great shaking, sifting and purifying work is going on among the people of God and the over-riding challenge to us all seems to be this: 'Don't miss your destiny!'

Shakespeare has Brutus address Cassius with these words:

> There is a tide in the affairs of men which taken at the flood leads on to fortune; omitted, all the voyage of their life is bound in shallows and in miseries. On such a full sea are we now afloat and we must take the current when it serves or lose our ventures.[16]

Could it be true, then, that we are at a special tide in the dealings of God with his church and his people throughout the world? I believe so.

Which of us would knowingly choose a future 'bound in shallows and in miseries'? Not one of us, surely? And yet this was the tragic decision made by Gehazi. The various blindspots he stumbled over led to his ultimate downfall and departure from the ministry which God had clearly intended for him. We pick up the narrative just after the spectacular healing of the leprous Syrian army commander, Naaman.

> Then Naaman and all his attendants went back to the man of God. He stood before him and said, 'Now I know that there is no God in all the world except in Israel. Please accept now a gift from your servant.'
>
> The prophet answered, 'As surely as the Lord lives, whom I serve, I will not accept a thing.' And even though Naaman urged him, he refused.
>
> 'If you will not,' said Naaman, 'please let me, your servant, be given as much earth as a pair of mules can carry, for your servant will never again make burnt offerings and sacrifices to any other god but the Lord. But may the Lord forgive your servant for this one thing: When my master enters the temple of Rimmon to bow down and he is leaning on my arm and I bow there also—when I bow down in the temple of Rimmon, may the Lord forgive your servant for this.'
>
> 'Go in peace,' Elisha said.
>
> After Naaman had travelled some distance, Gehazi, the servant of Elisha the man of God, said to himself, 'My master was too easy on Naaman, this Aramean, by not accepting from him what he brought. As surely as the Lord lives, I will run after him and get something from him.'
>
> So Gehazi hurried after Naaman. When Naaman saw him

running towards him, he got down from the chariot to meet him. 'Is everything all right?' he asked.

'Everything is all right,' Gehazi answered. 'My master sent me to say, "Two young men from the company of the prophets have just come to me from the hill country of Ephraim. Please give them a talent of silver and two sets of clothing."'

'By all means, take two talents,' said Naaman. He urged Gehazi to accept them and then tied up the two talents of silver in two bags, with two sets of clothing. He gave them to two of his servants and they carried them ahead of Gehazi. When Gehazi came to the hill, he took the things from the servants and put them away in the house. He sent the men away and they left. Then he went in and stood before his master Elisha.

'Where have you been, Gehazi?' Elisha asked.

'Your servant didn't go anywhere,' Gehazi answered.

But Elisha said to him, 'Was not my spirit with you when the man got down from his chariot to meet you? Is this the time to take money, or to accept clothes, olive groves, vineyards, flocks, herds or menservants and maidservants? Naaman's leprosy will cling to you and to your descendants for ever.' Then Gehazi went from Elisha's presence and he was leprous, as white as snow (2 Kings 5:15–27).

What are the challenges which confront us in these verses? Let me draw your attention to a number of them.

1. Unlike Gehazi, don't lose sight of the purpose of God for your life. When many young converts give their testimonies, either at their baptism or on other occasions when an evangelistic thrust is being given to the meeting, you will hear them say something like, 'And since I've been saved, my life has become filled with a real sense of *purpose.*' Have you ever been tempted, as I have, to stop the whole proceedings and ask them, 'What specific *purpose* is that?' I suspect that most Christians haven't got a clue what God's purpose is for their lives. I don't think Gehazi knew either.

At some point (we don't know when) Elisha had hand-picked Gehazi to be his servant, just as years before Elijah had in a similar way picked Elisha. From then on Gehazi had been a kind of 'right-hand man' to Elisha, a trusted disciple and carefully cultivated associate. Elisha had given various responsibilities to the promising newcomer, intending him to function alongside himself in most of the activities in which he was engaged. Gehazi must have had real gifts and great potential.

Most of us do not know when God is training and preparing us for our life's work. We are usually oblivious at the time to the fact that he is equipping us for the true function and ministry he ultimately has in mind for us. We may not, in fact, find that out for years. What we are presently involved in may seem so small, so trivial, so insignificant and so frustrating. Is this how it appeared to Gehazi as Elisha groomed him? 'Groomed him for what?' you may ask. I believe it was for no less a task than that of eventually becoming Elisha's successor and taking upon his shoulders (as Elisha had from Elijah) the mantle of prophet of Israel!

This may at first seem both astonishing and implausible, but an older writer, the German preacher F.W. Krummacher, has expressed it like this:

> The young man whose character now emerges and engages our attention, was not a neglected uncultivated being, picked from the dregs of the people. He must have received instruction from Elisha; his servant and companion in travel: and why may we not fairly suppose he was taken by him from the schools of the prophets? There is every probability of the kind, considering the previous employment by which Elisha himself is designated, namely as having 'poured water on the hands of Elijah' (2 Kings 3:11); considering, I say, the similar nature of Gehazi's employment in general, to that which had formerly belonged to the prophet Elisha... it can hardly be doubted that Elisha entertained high hopes respecting this spirited and evidently gifted young man.[17]

If this is so, then there is no indication that Gehazi was

fully clued up about the purpose of the special training in which he was currently engaged. The truth is, however, that God had a special purpose for him, just as he has for each one of us. We are being prepared to play our part in history. Consider, for example, the almost imperceptible aspects of preparation for prophethood which Gehazi unwittingly underwent. In 2 Kings 4:12–13 Elisha 'said to his servant Gehazi, "Call the Shunammite." So he called her, and she stood before him. Elisha said to him, "Tell her, 'You have gone to all this trouble for us. Now what can be done for you? Can we speak on your behalf to the king or the commander of the army?'"'

Why couldn't Elisha say all that himself? After all, the woman stood there in front of him too, so why bother relaying it all through Gehazi? Surely because Elisha is testing Gehazi's ability to relay word-for-word any message with which he is entrusted. And what is that but the prophetic task?

Similarly in 4:14 Elisha is seen coaching Gehazi in the use of his sensitivities and prophetic discernment of God's will when he asks his protégé, 'What can be done for her?' Even the so-called 'menial tasks' of simply running on Elisha's errands as messenger boy (4:26, 'Run to meet her and ask her, "Are you all right?"') are not to be lightly overlooked as of no significance whatsover in Gehazi's life. Later, a wonderful test is laid upon Gehazi when Elisha actually gives him a chance to try out his abilities in conveying God's power to the sick and needy when the older man hands over the staff of divine power and commissions Gehazi to convey the Lord's miraculous power to the dead child of the Shunammite woman (4:29 ff).

I don't believe Gehazi had a clue what was going on. The Lord often prefers it to be that way. He is watching us, proving us, testing us, and all in order to find out what is in us. God is looking for *faithfulness*. It is the number one factor in being entrusted with, and holding on to, any ministry from God.

In Luke 16:10–11 Jesus says some remarkably instructive words relating to this vital issue of *faithfulness:*

> Whoever can be trusted with very little can also be trusted with much, and whoever is dishonest with very little will also be dishonest with much. So if you have not been trustworthy in handling worldly wealth, who will trust you with true riches? And if you have not been trustworthy with someone else's property, who will give you property of your own?

How can you know when you are being tested for faithfulness? The answer is simple. Just notice what Jesus said and see that invariably you will be trusted with *little* before being promoted to *much*. You will handle the *material* before advancing to the *spiritual*. You will look after *someone else's* before being given *your own*. And that is a progression which cannot wisely be bypassed without landing either you or the church in trouble. Are you faithful in small tasks, the handling of money and property and the responsibilities temporarily delegated to you by your superiors? If not, you're unreliable and therefore not likely to see any further promotion in the work of the Lord.

Think of those tiring hours you've spent counselling the demanding needs of others, or those lessons for the children you've meticulously prepared. What about the drinks you've made and the mountain of cups you've washed up afterwards all out of love for that gang of rowdy youngsters? Then there's the open-air witness you've nervously turned up to, the books and tapes you're eagerly studying, and the often unexciting committee you're called to serve on. Yes, God is grooming you for something even if you don't yet know what it is. Will you be faithful? It's the first passport to future usefulness and promotion in the Lord's work.

How sad that Gehazi manifested early signs of his unfitness for the work. We notice his harshness and insensitivity to the poor distressed woman whose son had died (4:27, 'When she reached the man of God [Elisha] at the mountain, she took hold of his feet. Gehazi came over to push her away...'), and also the cold clinical professionalism with which he dealt with the dead child later on, 'Gehazi went on ahead and laid the staff on the boy's face, but there was no sound or response. So Gehazi went back to meet Elisha and told him, "The boy has not awakened"' (4:31).

There's none of the passion, single-minded determination, fervency and warm giving of self which was later to characterize Elisha's ministry to the dead body of the boy (4:32–35). Gehazi had failed, yes, but even when he clearly saw that he was devoid of a true serving heart and of the Holy Spirit's powerful anointing upon his life he was *content to stay that way*. Never once did he ask Elisha, 'Where did I go wrong?' He was indifferent to the responsibility of developing his gifts. He could not see the purpose of God for his life. But there's another equally disturbing factor which accounted for Gehazi's fall, a factor we too need to be challenged with.

2. Unlike Gehazi, don't lose sight of the presence of God in your life. Naaman had been marvellously healed. In a generous display of the nature of God's grace, Elisha had waived all remuneration and sent the Syrian home marvelling at the free kindness and mercy of Yahweh, the God of Israel. But Gehazi had other ideas.

Most of us are tested in one or more of three specific areas sooner or later. We will feel pressure come upon us in the realms of power, prosperity or purity—ambition, money or sex. At that point the issues are clear. Do we fear and love God more than these or will self and self-aggrandizement take first place in our lives? One American preacher was said to have regularly warned young seminarians and candidates for the ministry in words like these: 'Beware of a fall in the areas of greedy ambition, women or financial dishonesty—God may forgive you, but the people won't.' He was saying that a lapse in one or more of these areas can cause people to lose respect for both us and our ministry, and could ultimately mean our removal from it.

It is disturbing to watch Gehazi's conduct towards the foreign general, Naaman. In 2 Kings 5:20 he's talking to himself and referring contemptuously to Naaman as 'this Aramean'. 'My master was too easy on *this Aramean.*' It's obvious Gehazi viewed Naaman as a pagan, a foreign unbeliever to be 'milked'. To Gehazi's greedy eyes, Naaman is not someone that God simply wanted to bless for no charge. No, his heartless unfeeling mind moves in cold and calculating materialism devoid of the fear of God. 'As surely as the Lord lives,' he thinks, 'I will run after him and get something from him.' Gehazi's materialism and covetousness is revealed—all he can think of is his own financial security, monetary welfare, and a sizeable nest-egg for the future.

He even mocks Elisha's words when the latter refused the money in the first place. Elisha had said, 'As surely as the Lord lives, whom I serve, I will not accept a thing' (v.16). *'As surely as the Lord lives... I will!'* mocks Gehazi in sarcastic derision of Elisha's stupidity in looking a gift horse in the mouth. He mocks true spirituality for the sacrifices it makes and the seemingly unnecessary extremes to which it runs.

And so Gehazi is then found *lying,* first to Naaman, ('My Master has changed his mind', v.22), and then to Elisha his master ('Your servant didn't go anywhere', v.25). He was unconcerned about misrepresenting Elisha to the astonished Naaman and, worse still, didn't care what the effects of this would be on the new-found faith of the foreigner. Did Naaman show any disappointment as his 'illusions' about Elijah came crashing to the ground? Did he think, 'Ah well, men are men after all, and money is money'?

The silly story about the two scholars needing a talent of

silver and some new clerical dress must have sounded as hollow to Naaman's ears as it does to ours today.

Gehazi was unconcerned about the possibility of causing this new believer to stumble and of alienating him from his recently discovered faith. 'Salvation is *free*' said Elisha. 'Oh no it isn't!' said the mercenery, Gehazi. This dreadful loss of integrity meant that the writing was on the wall for the future ministry God had for this man. He didn't know that God sees all. The roof is off in all of our lives, and when we are more embarrassed that men know our secrets than that God does, then we stand in danger of a fall as devastating as that of Gehazi.

'God saw everything,' says the prophet in effect, when in verse 26 he rebukes his servant's deception. 'Was not my spirit with you when the man got down from his chariot to meet you?'

Another challenge came immediately upon the heels of this one. It was a challenge to Gehazi and it is also a challenge to us.

3. Unlike Gehazi, don't lose sight of the priorities of God for your life. 'Is this the time to take money, or to accept clothes, olive groves, vineyards, flocks, herds or menservants and maidservants?' (2 Kings 5:26).

Gehazi's ambitions sound large, expansive and visionary: plantations and flocks of domestic livestock with scores of servants to run the business; but what Elisha was saying is that his vision was too *small.* The times were too urgent and the call on his life too great for Gehazi to settle for anything less than that which God dictated as his true priorities. Life is precious. You and I have only got one life and it is too valuable to be squandered frivolously.

In one of his books Charles Swindoll sets before us the following scenario. Imagine your bank manager rang last Friday to inform you that an anonymous benefactor has selected you to be the privileged beneficiary of a wonderful new scheme. Every morning, starting today, he is to deposit into your bank account 86,400 pennies, that is

put his roots into temporal security and purely worldly ambitions. He was feathering his own nest and to hell with the kingdom of God! Here is the tragedy of a gifted and promising young man projecting himself into a life of ease, away from the church and withdrawn from the battle. All he envisaged was a life of peace and affluence in comfortable retirement on an ill-gotten pension. For this he abdicated the prophetic task and was put out of the Lord's service. 'For the love of money is a root of all kinds of evil. Some people, eager for money, have wandered from the faith and pierced themselves with many griefs' (1 Tim 6:10).

One last challenge comes with peculiar relevance to all of our lives as we draw to a conclusion our study of the rejection of Gehazi.

4. Unlike Gehazi, don't lose sight of the availability of the power of God in your life. Elisha pronounced God's judgement, 'Naaman's leprosy will cling to you and to your descendants for ever' (2 Kings 5:27a).

Gehazi was living in the middle of a supernatural move of God's Holy Spirit operating first in the ministry of Elijah, and, to an even greater degree latterly, in the ministry of his friend and mentor, Elisha.

He had seen poisoned waters healed, Moab defeated, a widow supplied with abundant oil, a barren womb conceive a child and later bring it to birth, that same child later raised from the dead, and, most recently, a leper totally cleansed from his hideous and disfiguring disease.

Gehazi lived in the middle of a flow of supernatural demonstrations of the kingdom of God, and yet he did not want this for his own life. It would take a great deal more than he had already seen to convince Gehazi that all of this was genuine. Here, then, was a man who quenched the fire of God's Spirit which would have burned so brightly in his life had he opened his mind and ministry to such possibilities. Somehow, none of what he was privileged to see registered upon the hardened heart of Gehazi, but served only to strengthen the resolve of his rebellion against God's will and his refusal to align his life with the divine destiny which stood within his grasp, had he but seized and embraced it. How fitting that it was *Naaman's* leprosy which came on this foolish rejector of God's power. It was so in Jesus' day that the rejection of the supernatural by both the secular and religious opponents of Jesus—kings, governors, Pharisees and Sadducees alike—returned on their own heads. 'The stone the builders rejected has become the capstone . . . a stone that causes men to stumble and a rock that makes them fall' (1 Pet 2:7–8).

We need to be very cautious and fearful in these days of astonishing displays of God's power in healings, deliverance, miracles, signs and wonders, and the restoration of the gifts of the Spirit to the body of Christ, that we don't imitate Gehazi in a swine-like treading of God's precious pearls of scriptural revelation under our feet. To do so may be to forfeit our ministry, to forfeit our destiny, to forfeit all that we presently hold dear. 'Then Gehazi went from Elisha's presence and he was leprous, as white as snow' (v.27b).

No longer fit for either the Lord's presence or the Lord's service, Gehazi lost everything worth having. He lost his health, his honour, his peace, his service, his ministry and even his ill-gotten wealth. The man who perhaps could have had a *triple* portion of the Spirit of Elijah had he become Elisha's successor (cf. 2 Kings 2:9–10), was doomed to forfeit all that and to rot out the end of his days as a leper, all because of his blindness, materialism and selfish ambition.

Unlike Gehazi, don't miss your destiny!

10

Ananias and Sapphira—Making Shipwreck of One's Faith

I once saw one of those 'Wayside Pulpit' billboards you sometimes pass outside the premises of churches and chapels. This one read, 'Don't let the possibility that the church is full of hypocrites put you off—there's always room for one more!' But if the passage we're going to look at next tells us anything, it tells us that there is no room for hypocrites within the church and that their presence invites the judgement of God, often in astonishing severity.

The story of what happened to Ananias and Sapphira has puzzled and disturbed most people who've paused to consider the seriousness of it. Both of them dropped dead, one after the other, when the piercing eyes and stern voice of the Apostle Peter confronted them boldly after what, to us, seems by no means an exceptional display of hypocrisy. It concerned the matter of their giving to the funds of the early church. Coming immediately after the wonderful displays of power and generosity which Luke records as typical of the day-to-day life of the early church (Acts 4:32–37), it reminds us that the foul breath of hell can blow through *any* church and leave its stinking after-effects on the lives of some, eventually causing us all to shudder at the possible outcome. The perfect church doesn't exist this side of heaven. We all know that. But we do not want to resign ourselves to the inevitability of having an Ananias and Sapphira in our midst if we can possibly avoid it.

> Now a man named Ananias, together with his wife Sapphira, also sold a piece of property. With his wife's full knowledge he kept back part of the money for himself, but brought the rest and put it at the apostles' feet.
>
> Then Peter said, 'Ananias, how is it that Satan has so filled your heart that you have lied to the Holy Spirit and have kept for yourself some of the money you received for the land? Didn't it belong to you before it was sold? And after it was sold, wasn't the money at your disposal? What made you think of doing such a thing? You have not lied to men but to God.'
>
> When Ananias heard this, he fell down and died. And great fear seized all who heard what had happened. Then the young men came forward, wrapped up his body, and carried him out and buried him. About three hours later his wife came in not knowing what had happened. Peter asked her, 'Tell me, is this the price you and Ananias got for the land?'
>
> 'Yes,' she said, 'that is the price.'
>
> Peter said to her, 'How could you agree to test the Spirit of the Lord? Look! The feet of the men who buried your husband are at the door, and they will carry you out also.'
>
> At that moment she fell down at his feet and died. Then the young men came in and, finding her dead, carried her out and buried her beside her husband. Great fear seized the whole church and all who heard about these events (Acts 5:1–11).

The first disturbing fact which confronts us about this couple is that they were evidently regarded as believers. We have no real reason to doubt this, and even the way in which their sin is described: 'You have lied to the Holy Spirit' (v.3), and, 'You agreed to test the Spirit of the Lord,' seems to underline the most alarming yet basic assumption of the incident—that these two people were related in some vital and intimate way to the Holy Spirit. So that when we ask, 'Is it possible for a Christian to perpetrate an act of deliberate deception?', the example of Ananias and Sapphira is meant to answer that question in the affirmative: 'Yes, he or she may certainly do so; despicable though such an action may be.'

But in my judgement, the most shocking fact to emerge from this incident is something even more distressing than this dreadful possibility. It is what Peter asserts to be the true explanation of how such a thing could have happened. 'Satan has so filled your heart that you have lied to the Holy Spirit' (v.3); a shockingly accurate analysis which we must struggle to understand because it exposes a great deal of what goes on in perhaps a disguised way beneath the surface of many churches. It also explains why so many terrible lapses occur among the genuine people of God. What is this shocking explanation? It is this: *a Christian can, to some degree, so align himself with Satan's cause that he can become infiltrated by the forces of darkness or, to use the terminology of the New Testament itself, he can become 'demonized'*.

Now please note I said '*demonized*' and not '*demon possessed*'. Not only is the latter expression an unbiblical one, it is also grossly misleading, especially when used in connection with a believer. The term 'demon possessed' is used in many English versions of the New Testament to translate the various phrases used in the Greek which refer to people being infiltrated by demons. But this is not strictly an accurate translation. To quote from a leading authority in this field:

> In the original Greek text there are three expressions normally used to describe the influence of demons—
> 1) to *have* an unclean Spirit (Matthew 11:18, Mark 7:25, Luke 8:27)
> 2) to *be in* an evil spirit (Mark 1:23, Mark 5:2, The English preposition 'with' is the Greek preposition 'en')
> 3) to be demonized (Greek: daimonizomenoi Matthew 4:24, 8:16, 8:28, 8:33, 9:32, Mark 1:32, 5:15, 16, 18, Luke 8:36).[18]

The Greek verb which means 'to be demonized', however, is consistently mistranslated in the King James Bible, which inserts the term 'demon possessed', a translation which is as unfortunate as it is inaccurate. A far more reasonable translation could be rendered by the use of English words such as 'afflicted', or 'infiltrated' or even 'oppressed'.

Possession clearly implies complete ownership in the sense that a person has become the property of another. It is impossible for a believer to be anybody's property, in an ultimate sense, other than the property of the Lord. That is why to speak of believers being 'demon *possessed*' is dangerously inaccurate. It says too much. It puts into question the radical nature of the new birth and the full reality of our re-creation in Christ (2 Cor 5:17). Equally dangerous, however, is so majoring upon the truths and realities of our position in Christ as to become blinded to the possibility of the kind of things which Satan may do, even to genuine Christian believers, if he is given the space and the opportunity to do so. It is out of a sober appreciation of the latter that I'm forced to the conclusion that a Christian may be demonized, often to a very severe degree, and that this is exactly what happened to Ananias and Sapphira. And if that scares you, I want you to know that it scares me too.

Ananias and Sapphira warn us. They stand like beacons on those rocky outcrops within shallow waters, alerting us to the hidden dangers below which could make shipwreck of our lives if we were foolish enough to venture upon them. It is not only possible for a believer to lapse severely into an immoral act of some kind, but it is also possible that he may at the same time open the door of his life to a severe degree of domination by evil forces; and, furthermore, one possible outcome of this condition may be for God not only to terminate that believer's ministry for good, but also to terminate prematurely his life, removing him from this earthly scene for ever.

It was the Apostle Paul who, when writing some severe words to the church at Corinth about the scandalous goings-on at some of their communion services, went on to explain the mysterious sicknesses and deaths that had occurred in the church:

> For anyone who eats and drinks without recognising the body of the Lord eats and drinks judgment on himself. That is why many among you are weak and sick, and a number of you have fallen asleep [i.e. died] (1 Cor 11:29–30).

In 1 Corinthians 5, Paul gave his directions as to how to proceed in one particularly notorious case of immorality which had sprung up within the Corinthian congregation. A man was actually living in an incestuous relationship with his father's wife; most probably she was his own stepmother (1 Cor 5:1). Paul calls for a united action on the part of the church and its leadership. The man is to be solemnly expelled from the membership and fellowship of the church. The peculiar phraseology Paul used to describe what this would entail is in verse 5: 'Hand this man over to Satan, so that the sinful nature may be destroyed and his spirit saved on the day of the Lord.'

Opinions differ, of course, as to what these words mean, but at the very least Paul envisages that in being expelled from the church the man enters Satan's territory and comes under Satan's power, and as it were falls within his vile clutches at least to some degree. This is a disciplinary measure designed to issue in positive results. Although 2 Corinthians 2:4–11 makes clear that this particular individual was both restored to the Lord and to the church not long after the reception of Paul's first letter, it is more than a possibility that the words 'that the sinful nature [or flesh] may be destroyed and his spirit saved on the day of the Lord' here in 1 Corinthians 5:5 imply that the man could have died. Radical treatment indeed for a sin which was so abhorrent it even scandalized the pagan world (1 Cor 5:1)!

There are other believers, in the pages of the New Testament, who 'make shipwreck' of their lives. For example, consider those words of the Apostle Paul in 1 Timothy 1:19–20, 'Some have rejected these [faith and a good conscience] and so have *shipwrecked* their faith. Among them are Hymenaeus and Alexander, whom I have handed over to Satan to be taught not to blaspheme.' There is evidently a progression here from the backsliding of Peter, and even from the castaway condition of a Gehazi. These people have been *shipwrecked*, a sin with its attendant consequences which, though it falls short of complete apostasy, nevertheless leaves us shuddering at the depths to which these pitiable individuals have sunk in their mad voyage to 'freedom' from the restraints of God's will and God's word.

There is a high-handed wilfulness entailed in becoming a shipwreck which may not be so in the case of those who are backsliding. Paul says they have 'rejected' faith and a good conscience: they have wilfully jettisoned those things. Any rocks which they have subsequently struck, they seemed to have headed for quite deliberately. The wilful nature of their sin is brought out in some of the other things the Apostle tells us about them. Their 'consciences have been seared' (1 Tim 4:2) by advocating the teachings they now hold. They have gone against the Holy Spirit's promptings and his constraints. Like doppelgangers of the Apostle Paul, many former evangelists are now destroying the faith they once sought to preach (see Galatians 1:23). Yet in some cases it is difficult to say that these men were not, or are not still, genuine believers, even though their lives presently appear wrecked upon the rocks of infidelity and unbelief.

Paul says that Hymenaeus and Alexander had lapsed into 'blasphemy' (1 Tim 1:20). This cannot be the blasphemy against the Holy Spirit, otherwise Paul would not have held out any hope for their recovery (see Matthew 12:31), nor envisaged a time when they would have 'learned not to' do it. What is described here is the bitter and shocking things which backslidden people say about spiritual things. Like the vile enemies of the faith Jude spoke of so vehemently, these shipwrecked saints may 'speak abusively against whatever they do not understand' (Jude 10). For a long while their life may be totally debased and undesirable. It's still Hymenaeus Paul has in mind when he writes again to Timothy in 2 Timothy 2:16–18 of those who indulged in 'godless chatter' and became more and more 'ungodly' as they 'wandered away from the truth'.

The late Paul Tillich, a respected theologian in some circles, who taught systematic theology at Union Theological Seminary for many years, was a man who had previously abandoned his wife and fathered several illegitimate children by his mistress while at the same time teaching a rising generation of ministers the theology he believed they would need in order to perform their task and life calling. Alexander also appears again in 2 Timothy 4:14 where he is said to have done the Apostle Paul 'a great deal of harm'. Timothy is to guard against his despicable influence, for as the Apostle explains 'he strongly opposed our message'.

Now you may doubt whether genuine believers can go this far. But I am personally sure that it is so. The late Professor R. V. G. Tasker was once avowedly liberal in his theology and therefore an opponent of what many scathingly dub as 'evangelical fundamentalism'. While teaching New Testament at London University, he attended Dr Lloyd-Jones' famous series of Friday night Bible studies at Westminster Chapel. The outcome of this was quite wonderful. Not only was Professor Tasker restored to a thoroughly conservative scholarship with regard to the New Testament, he also went on to edit the world-renowned series of New Testament commentaries published by Inter-Varsity Press—the Tyndale New Testament Commentaries. Of course, I am not implying that Tasker was ever in the same category as Hymenaeus and Alexander, but I would still cite him as an illustration of one who can drift far from a full-orbed biblical faith and yet be restored.

Paul said he had handed these men over to Satan (1 Tim 1:20) so that they may be 'taught not to blaspheme', ie *paideuthosin*, a verb closely related to the one used in Hebrews 12:6–7 and carrying the meaning of 'taught by chastening'. Here, then, is the 'severe mercy' of God which refuses to let his wayward children go, even if their ultimate restoration entails the most serious forms of chastening, including painful loss, bodily affliction and perhaps even death.

This rather lengthy digression from Ananias and Sapphira has been both necessary and important to establish something of the consistent New Testament teaching concerning those who stand in danger of making 'shipwreck' of their faith, and for the corroboration and additional light which these examples throw upon the difficult case of Ananias and Sapphira.

When we ask how Ananias and Sapphira could stoop to the extent of 'lying to the Holy Spirit', it is clear that in their lives, as in the life of Judas also, it was not an involuntary action. Satan did not 'fill their heart' either by surprise or by sudden invasion. Satan has no rights whatsoever over a believer, and certainly not to dominate our thinking or our behaviour unless we have previously taken the prior step of *giving him permission* to do so. There must be some willing co-operation on our part. Satan cannot just lie in ambush as it were, and 'jump on our back' whenever it suits him. This can only happen by our giving him permission to do so.

The steps by which Satan got a hold upon Ananias and Sapphira are fairly obvious.

1. Jealousy and envy

It was such jealousy which caused Cain to murder Abel,

only here it was not a case of *murder* but of *suicide*. They became envious of Joseph Barnabas and the prominence he enjoyed in the church due to his great liberality, his evident spiritual gifts and his powerful spiritual dynamic (Acts 4:36–37). Ananias watched the promotion of Joseph up the 'ecclesiastical ladder' and he and his wife decided that they wanted 'a piece of the action'. This envy in turn gave way to

2. Carnal ambition

It must have sickened them both to see Joseph become the 'blue-eyed boy' in the life of the early church, even to the point of being nicknamed 'Barnabas'—'Son of Encouragement'. Desiring the same popularity, Ananias and Sapphira contrived a plan to edge their way into the apostles' 'good books'. It is possible to be both back-slapping and backsliding at the same time. If Joseph could go and 'sell a field', they could match that and 'sell a piece of property' (Acts 5:1). When Joseph 'brought the money . . . and put it at the apostles' feet', they could ape this action to a degree and, after taking their cut, they 'brought the rest and put it at the apostles' feet' (v.2). They copied in their devious way the *deeds* of Barnabas, but lacked totally his *disposition*.

3. Lying

As with Gehazi, we see here the complete loss of integrity entailed in their actions. They must have discussed together and then rationalized the whole business until they came to the point where they could justify with their minds what their consciences told them was wrong. They were living a lie and they knew it. They struck a bargain with sin and thought that God would approve of the deal. They pretended to give all, but deliberately kept back a good proportion of the whole, and thought they could bluff Peter, and therefore the Lord, with their hypocrisy. Their holiness was, at this point, only skin deep. Their sin was not that they didn't give every penny ('After it was sold wasn't the money at your disposal?' v.4), but that in handing the money over, they pretended that they had. It was the sin of deliberate deception.

4. Avarice

The desire to be or to stay rich is always a trap and a snare (1 Tim 6:10), and it's the devil who sets that particular trap. At some point in this downward regression, Satan got in. His demons exploited the 'door of opportunity' flung open for them by the duplicity of Ananias and Sapphira. Satan is called in the Bible 'Baalzebub' or 'Lord of the flies' because like flies on a dunghill or maggots on a corpse, he and his minions always gather wherever they can smell the stench of corruption. Lives steeped in hypocrisy will quickly become fly-blown with the maggots of hell, and no place gives Satan more pleasure to go about his terrifying work of demonic infiltration than the life of a carnal Christian.

'How is it that Satan has *so filled* your heart?' asked Peter (v.3). Christian people were never intended to be houses merely swept clean of Satan's former habitation.

If the Holy Spirit isn't filling our hearts, a filling which issues in a lifestyle that keeps in step with the Spirit (Eph 5:18; Gal 5:25), then be warned, something else will. 'Nature abhors a vacuum' and so does the devil. He wants the opportunity to return to the house from which he was once evicted (Lk 11:24–26). The tragedy here was two-fold. Not only are we confronted with the fact that Satan had once again begun to hold sway in the heart of Ananias, but also that he did so *with Ananias' consent*. Ananias' heart became filled with a very unholy spirit indeed.

There are three principal doors of entry for demonic oppression and infiltration within the life of a believer.

1. Grievous or traumatic experiences which are not

handled correctly and which may leave us open to attack by spirits of fear (often in the form of various recognizable phobias), spirits of depression, and lying spirits of rejection.

2. The indulgence of carnal desires or the sins of the flesh. Demonic spirits can 'climb on the back' of such sins and bring the believer into bondage in the areas of either certain emotions like envy, lust, pride, hatred and bitterness, or carnal practices from which it is very difficult to break free (drug addiction, sexual immorality or perversion, outbursts of rage, stealing, lying, quarrelsomeness and so on). Any of the 'works of the flesh' listed in Galatians 5:19–28 may become the occasion of demonic bondage if wilfully indulged by the believer. With Ananias and Sapphira, it was of course a lying spirit which latched onto their deliberate deception.

3. Any involvement with psychic, clairvoyant, mediumistic or occult practices. Examples would include astrology, fortune-telling, ESP, hypnotism, spiritualism, tarot, witchcraft, psychometry, ouija, fantasy games such as 'Dungeons and Dragons', and an unhealthy interest in Eastern religions or the so-called 'Christian' cults which deviate seriously from biblical orthodoxy, for example, Yoga, TM, Mormonism and Jehovah's Witnesses.

All these forbidden attitudes or practices, if deliberately indulged and persisted in, can open a door to Satan and provide him with the opportunity to seduce, blind and terrorize the wayward believer and so hold him in a grip which needs to be authoritatively broken by genuine repentance and deliverance ministered in the name of Jesus.

As we saw with Gehazi, the outstanding characteristics of believers in this kind of trouble are the boldness with which their sin is carried out, together with the mistaken certainty that no one could ever find out. Ananias and Sapphira even persuaded themselves that somehow God himself had become blind, deaf and dumb; a God who could see nothing, hear nothing and was incapable of properly exposing it even if he did. But, as William Gurnall has written, 'Hypocrisy is too thin a veil to blind the eyes of the Almighty.' The sin of Ananias and Sapphira was uncovered *supernaturally* in that prophetic insight was granted to the Apostle Peter. The Lord Jesus who knew by this same gift that the woman of Samaria had had five husbands (Jn 4) imparted this ability to his servant Peter.

How wonderful that this is a gift still available to the whole body of Christ up to this day as 1 Corinthians 14:24–25 makes clear:

> But if an unbeliever or someone who does not understand comes in while everybody is prophesying, he will be convinced by all that he is a sinner and will be judged by all, and the secrets of his heart will be laid bare.

At the same time it would appear that Peter operated in another gift of the Holy Spirit, namely, the 'distinguishing of spirits' (1 Cor 12:10) which enabled him to recognize the direct activity of Satan secretly operating under the sinful conduct of this pitiful couple. Such was the degree of anointing that not only were two people singled out and named as the culprits from a church consisting of over 5,000 members, but also the exact nature of their sin was exposed, so that others could take note and be warned. The absence of such gifts from the church for so long has meant that if God were to judge with similar severity in our churches today the proportion of deaths would probably be much higher. Furthermore, not only have characters like Ananias and Sapphira remained unmasked within our churches, but we in our foolishness would have given them a vote of thanks at the church AGM and at least made them house-group leaders by now!

Someone once asked, 'If the world despises a hypocrite, what must they think of him in heaven?' What indeed! Verses 4–10 in Acts 5 help supply the answer. We cannot but be struck by the severity of God's action. This sets in our minds the healthy reminder that the more alive our churches become to the presence and power of God, then the more acute and uncompromising will be the Lord's dealings with us. A. W. Tozer once pointed out that 'when hypocrites ran up against Jesus it was like a cat running into a mowing machine'. It was Isaiah's experience in the presence of a holy God that he felt himself 'ruined' (Is 6:5), or in modern terms, 'disintegrated'. It was as though he had come apart at the seams. One modern author has expressed the state to which Isaiah was rendered like this:

> In a brief second he was exposed, made naked beneath the gaze of the absolute standard of holiness . . . the instant he measured himself by the ultimate standard he was destroyed —morally and spiritually annihilated. He was undone. He came apart. His sense of integrity collapsed.[19]

Ananias and Sapphira were to have both their ministries and their lives instantly terminated. They had, to some significant degree, aligned themselves with Satan and so forfeited to that same extent the protection of Jesus. Those who 'make shipwreck' of their faith always do; and therefore they open their lives to enemy attack in the forms of sickness, misery, chastening and even death. (Look again at 1 Timothy 1:19–20, 1 Corinthians 5:5 and 11:30.)

It was C. H. Spurgeon who said: 'Nothing is to be despised more than a mere painted fire, the simulation of earnestness. Sooner let us have an honest death than a counterfeit life.'

Terminal chastening still remains one option which God may choose when we have refused to respond to the less severe forms of his confrontation with our sins. It is as though some believers yield themselves so much to the powers of darkness and the destructive influences of sin that God mercifully removes them before they can do any further damage either to themselves or others. Perhaps some sins border so closely upon the unforgivable sin of apostasy that God permits the drastic chastening of death to intervene in order to save such Christians from *total* disaster. Is this what Paul meant when he said, 'That the sinful nature may be destroyed and his spirit saved on the day of the Lord' (1 Cor 5:5)?

If so, it would shed more light upon that passage in 1 Corinthians 3 where the Apostle speaks of the judgement of Christ testing the works of all believers and especially his ministers, with the outcome that for some individuals their works subsequent to salvation will be burned up as so much 'wood, hay or straw'. Are such people saved? Yes, says Paul, 'He himself will be saved, but only as one escaping through the flames' (v.15), or as we would put it today, they seem to 'squeak' into heaven by 'the skin of their teeth'. We are not saved by our good works. Good works are, however, vitally important in the determination of our rewards (Eph 2:8–10, 2 Cor 5:10). The works of some Christians will be burned up. They will thus forfeit their rewards, but not their salvation. Premature death may remove certain believers from the possibility of serving him on earth any more.

It is no wonder that 'great fear seized the whole church and all who heard about these events' (v.11). We, too, need to recover in the church this fear of God if we are to press on in true discipleship. The cost of going on with God is great, but the cost of not going on with God is greater. Even the outside world watched these events in respectful silence so that 'no-one else dared j in them' (v.13). The realization of the truth which Peter later expressed in one of his epistles had dawned upon them all: 'It is time for judgement to begin with the family of God; and if it begins with us, what will the outcome be for those who do not obey the gospel of God?' (1 Pet 4:17).

There has been talk in recent years concerning the prospect of raising that ill-fated ship, the Titanic, which sank during her maiden voyage to New York in April

1912. Whether this extraordinary enterprise will ever be accomplished, I don't know, but such a task seems mere child's play when compared with the difficulty of retrieving from shipwreck a life which, though once keen and zealous for God, has now fallen under God's chastening because it threatens to defile the work of the Lord, corrupt the lives of others, or bring God's glory down into the gutter before the eyes of a watching world.

The lives of Ananias and Sapphira shine like a lighthouse on a stormy night, beaming out their solemn warning to all generations: 'Beware all who sail here!' Wise Christians will take heed and resolve to plot a very different course from theirs. Becoming a shipwreck is not an option any of us would willingly choose.

11

Judas—the Mystery of Apostasy

The alarming scriptures we have already considered (Heb 6, Heb 10 and the parables of the drag net and the sower) have demonstrated very clearly the possibility of a person fitting for some time within a fellowship of genuine believers and yet never truly belonging among them. The supreme example of such a well-disguised misfit is, of course, Judas Iscariot. He is the most clearly-delineated example in Scripture of what it means to be an apostate, and we are going to look now at how the Scriptures themselves go a long way to explain what happened to him.

> Then Judas Iscariot, one of the Twelve, went to the chief priests to betray Jesus to them. They were delighted to hear this and promised to give him money. So he watched for an opportunity to hand him over (Mk 14:10–11).

It is plain that Judas was able to move freely within the inner circle of Jesus' closest disciples for the space of three years, and that no one (with the exception of Jesus) was able to detect his true status and heart condition. In some ways the presence of Judas served the purpose of advancing God's ultimate plans and intentions, and nothing he did could take the Lord by surprise. When people ask,

'Where does God's sovereignty end and man's free will begin?' then the history of Judas vividly pictures for us the responsible choices men make in their sphere of freedom, and yet at the same time forces us to realize that such choices operate under the umbrella of the over-arching and sovereign purposes of God. Luis Palau once expressed the truth powerfully and memorably in this way: 'God's sovereignty never ends, and man's free will only begins where God says it begins and ends where God says it should end.' There is a mysterious interplay of the human and the divine in what happened to Judas. And yet the riddle of how he could have committed such acts as he did is compounded by five factors.

1. Judas had known a great change in his life because of Christ and still he was lost. Who was Judas? Scholars have debated the likely background from which he came. Some have argued that the name 'Iscariot' means 'Of the Sicarri'. The 'Sicarri' were the 'dagger men', a nickname given to one of the many anti-Roman terrorist groups which proliferated in the enemy-occupied Palestine of Jesus' day. Such groups infiltrated crowds and in the confusion of the pressing multitudes would plunge stiletto-daggers between the ribs of any Roman soldiers present at the time. Hence the nickname. Don't be surprised that Jesus took such a man within the circle of the Twelve. Simon the *Zealot* was also a rabidly anti-Roman terrorist, whereas Levi (or Matthew) was a corrupt, pro-Roman official who collected taxes for the government. Most of Jesus' disciples had unsavoury personal records which they then left behind upon their association with him.

Judas had apparently put all this behind him for the last three years, and to all appearances had taken his rightful place amid those whose lives had been radically changed through their knowledge of Jesus. The question this raises however is, 'Just how radical had that change been?'

2. Judas had felt a great admiration for Christ and still he was lost. In the immediate context (Mk 14:1–11) we read of Judas' disgruntled complaint, voiced sourly in the presence of Jesus on the occasion of the woman anointing Jesus with an expensive jar of ointment. But until this incident happened, we would not have picked up so much as a hint of animosity, discontent, hatred or even dislike in the heart of Judas towards his Master. There is every reason for assuming the contrary, namely, that Judas had shared a similar esteem, admiration and affection for Jesus as that of the other eleven disciples. After all, he'd spent frequent nights with them, living homeless under the starry skies; he'd given up whatever roots and security he possessed in order to follow Jesus, and he'd walked many foot-weary journeys in ministry, and been dubbed a heretic and trouble-maker along with Jesus and the other disciples. Only admiration for Jesus could explain such loyalty for this length of time, but the question remains, 'Was this admiration for the Master enough?'

3. Judas had shared in great company with Christ and still he was lost. He was 'one of the Twelve'. He had kept company with good men, believing men, and spiritual men, and all that time he had been quite indistinguishable from them in both his speech and actions. At the Last Supper, when Jesus announced, 'One of you is going to betray me,' it is significant that no one responded, 'We know who that is! Judas! I knew it all along . . . never did quite fit . . . stood out like a sore thumb . . . inevitable he'd do something like this!' No, they all said, 'Lord is it I?' If I may put it like this, Judas gave every appearance of being a genuine Christian, and so each of the disciples trusted *him* more than they trusted *their own hearts*.

Being at every meeting and fitting in well with the crowd of Jesus' genuine followers guarantees nothing. The company you keep may be truly godly, but does that prove that you're godly too? I think not.

4. Judas had heard a great deal of Christ's preaching and still he was lost. There are ignorant people who, if they ever hear Christian preaching, respond unhesitatingly with the verdict: 'Rubbish! Myths and fairy tales! Not for me thank you very much.' But this wasn't Judas. Like so many today in our churches, Judas heard waggon-loads of sermons, and even sat under the most anointed preaching human ears were ever privileged to hear. The Sermon on the Mount, the magnificent parables, the discourses recorded in John's gospel, the wonderful teaching in the Upper Room (Jn 13–17), all of these were almost daily fare for Judas. He must have admired the authority of the Preacher, the precision of his logic and arguments, the beauty of his illustrations, and the faithfulness of his application to the needs and circumstances of the crowds of hearers which Jesus always drew.

All of this may be so with others too, and to such a degree that a person even perceives the truth of Christ's word and the principles of his teaching. And yet the most we can say for such a one is that like Judas, the only end achieved by all this has been to render *without excuse* their subsequent apostasy from the Lord.

5. Judas witnessed great demonstrations of the Spirit's power through Christ and still he was lost. Judas was there to see nearly every sign and wonder which Jesus ever performed. With his own eyes he'd seen leprosy banished and wholeness restored; he'd seen demons run in craven surrender to Jesus' authority; he'd seen sightless eyes beam with the excitement of restored vision, he'd seen lifeless limbs creatively restored to new vigour and strength; he'd seen the hostile forces of wind and waves hushed to silence with a word of command and he'd seen corpses rise to renewed life once again at Jesus' word.

More than this, Judas had himself been delegated with similar authority to perform equally powerful demonstrations of the kingdom of God. (Matthew 10:1, 'He called his twelve disciples to him and gave them authority to drive out evil spirits and to cure every kind of disease and sickness.') He probably returned from such missions just as delighted as the rest that God could have used him in such a way (Lk 10:17) to overthrow the work of the evil one in the lives of men and women.

All this amounted to conclusive proof of the identity of Jesus and the truth of his mission. But such is the blackness and complicated treachery of sin that none of this was sufficient to uproot sin's hold on the innermost heart and soul of Judas.

No reformation of life, education of mind, inspiration of truth, influence of example, or demonstration of power is sufficient in and of itself to convert a man or woman. Judas had to repudiate a great deal of light in order to make his suicidal plunge into hell, but repudiate it he did. Why?

In recent years such playwrights as Dennis Potter (*Son of Man*), novelists and historians like Frank Yerby and Hugh Schonfield, film-makers and musical directors (the TV series *Jesus of Nazareth* and stage musical *Jesus Christ Superstar* are but two examples of the kind of work I have in mind) have all sought to one degree or another to exonerate Judas and whitewash his character, accusing the gospel writers of distortion and slander and even going so far as to imply or assert that Judas was the only man with integrity amid the whole group of Jesus' disciples. Certainly the astonishing course and conduct of Judas requires some explanation. But sin is, at basis, totally irrational and perhaps a completely satisfying solution as to why Judas behaved as he did, will for ever elude us.

Four steps to Judas' downfall

1. The disappointment he felt

'Then Judas Iscariot . . . went to the chief priests.' When? Immediately after Jesus had rebuked his critical spirit: 'Leave her alone . . . why are you bothering her?' (Mk 14:6). Some would-be disciples intensely dislike the correction and rebuke which God's word brings into their lives. They soon take offence at 'close' preaching and speaking.

Furthermore, Jesus had promised the disciples dazzling rewards for following him (Mark 10:29–30, 'A hundred times as much in this present age') and even thrones for them to sit on (Mt 19:28); but this had not been realized in exactly the same way that Judas and the rest had anticipated. Instead of riding into Jerusalem on a white charger, overthrowing Rome and setting up the Messianic kingdom, Jesus had spoken repeatedly of his death (Mk 8:31; 9:31) mounted an unattractive beast of burden (Mk 11:1–11) and set out an entirely different programme of world conquest involving much delay, difficulty and disappointment (Mk 13). Quite frankly, Jesus was not all that Judas had hoped he would be.

A man can only be disappointed with the Lord's way if he thinks his own way is better. 'I did it my way' is not only the avowed life philosophy of every fallen son of Adam, it's also the secret agenda of many would-be disciples. Inevitably God's programme of trials, sufferings and surprising uphill struggles prove a disappointment to them, as they did to Judas. Judas became a disappointed and disillusioned man.

2. The company he preferred

Judas felt increasingly the discomfort of keeping up appearances and spending time with the rest. It was all to come to a head in the upper room when, shamed into the open, Judas left that intimate gathering and went out into the night (Jn 13:30). When a man prefers the company of Jesus' enemies to that of Jesus' friends the writing is on the wall as to the direction he is taking with his life.

3. The covetousness he indulged

They 'promised to give him money' (v.11). The complaints made by Judas over the 'waste of money' at the anointing of Jesus' head (Mk 14:5) were actually rooted in gross materialism and a lack of integrity in the area of finances. 'He was a thief . . . he used to help himself to what was put into [the bag]' (Jn 12:6). Is it any wonder, then, that the conversation with the chief priests took the course which it did? 'What are you willing to give me if I hand him over to you?' (Mt 26:15). And the paltry sum of thirty pieces of silver agreed to as payment for betrayal (the price of a handicapped or senile old slave), exposes the mean-minded condition of Judas' covetous heart. He loved money. And through the narrow chink of one undealt-with vice, the sin of apostasy was to enter in. There's nothing too complex about apostasy. The devil took him captive because of the foothold he gained through one lust which Judas had successfully rationalized and defended. At first Judas may have loved the truth, but at bottom he loved money *more*. And as Esau traded his birthright for a bowl of steaming hot soup, so Judas and people like him forfeit all that God has for them by selling off their Christian profession, just as cheaply as Esau did, to Satan's highest bidder.

4. The compact he made

'So he watched for an opportunity to hand him over' (v.11). Judas had secretly surrendered his mind and spirit to the devil. He would now play the part of a totally co-operative agent in Satan's hands: 'Then Satan entered Judas' (Lk 22:3). Again, 'the devil had already prompted Judas Iscariot . . . to betray Jesus . . . as soon as Judas took the bread, Satan entered into him' (Jn 13:2, 27).

There is no neutrality. We either belong to the Lord or else the devil will claim us as his property to use as he wishes. You are either in covenant with the Lord or with Satan; either Jesus reigns in your life or Satan does.

Potential apostates never see it like this. Viewing themselves as the captain of the ship of their own fate and masters of their own destiny, they never realize that there is no such thing as neutrality, feigned or otherwise, in the

Christian life. Consequently they never beseech Jesus to save and rescue them; they're never shocked enough by the reality of Satan's power to make a break with that deceiver and throw themselves on the mercy of King Jesus. In spite of all appearances the apostate has never changed sides, he has never *totally defected* from Satan's empire. His presence among God's people is rather more in the capacity of a fifth columnist than that of true faith commitment. The changes in Judas' life were purely cosmetic ones. His was a life never utterly surrendered to the Lord.

The shock of Judas' departure never seems to have totally left the rest of the disciples. You'll recall that even after the resurrection and ascension of Jesus, Luke records how the 120 gathered in the upper room awaiting the promised Holy Spirit (Acts 1:12–20). Among the many fascinating insights we can gain from the Scriptures into what occurred during this ten-day period before Pentecost, is the light these verses throw upon the apostasy of Judas. Verses 15–20 are particularly relevant:

> In those days Peter stood up among the believers (a group numbering about a hundred and twenty) and said, 'Brothers, the Scripture had to be fulfilled which the Holy Spirit spoke long ago through the mouth of David concerning Judas, who served as guide for those who arrested Jesus—he was one of our number and shared in this ministry.'
>
> (With the reward he got for his wickedness, Judas bought a field; there he fell headlong, his body burst open and all his intestines spilled out. Everyone in Jerusalem heard about this, so they called that field in their language Akeldama, that is, Field of Blood.)
>
> 'For,' said Peter, 'it is written in the book of Psalms, "May his place be deserted; let there be no-one to dwell in it," and, "May another take his place of leadership."'

Clearly, as the disciples prayed and meditated together, much of their thinking was focused upon Psalms 69 and 109. Psalm 69 was particularly appropriate on this occasion. In verses 16–21 the psalmist predicts and describes in detail some of the sufferings of Jesus. (Considering the shock such sufferings had induced in the Twelve, it is little wonder they sought to fit the facts of Jesus' passion and death into the prophetic framework of Scripture taken as a whole.) Psalm 69:29–36 confidently predicts the triumphs of the gospel in the church and in the world and would have served to awaken faith for the intended mission which the Pentecostal baptism in the Spirit was designed to both fire and inspire. But sandwiched between these two sections of the Psalm, in verses 22–28, are some astonishing statements which gave Peter and the rest the breakthrough in revelation that they needed to answer the question: 'Why was Judas lost?'

Acts 1:17 is particularly poignant. Peter there expresses the acutely painful horror felt by all of them at the apostasy of Judas: 'He was one of *our* number and shared in *this* ministry.' The unspoken words which lie beneath the surface are: 'How could he do such a thing? What on earth went wrong with Judas? What happened to him?'

The consoling answers to some of these questions were discovered in Psalm 69. And as Peter says, Judas' conduct was the fulfilment of Scripture: 'Brothers, the Scripture had to be fulfilled which the Holy Spirit spoke long ago through the mouth of David *concerning Judas*, who served as a guide for those who arrested Jesus' (Acts 1:16). If you take the trouble to read the aforementioned verses of Psalm 69 they disclose the following facts:

1. The Last Supper was the occasion when God's judgement fell irrevocably upon Judas: 'May the table set before them become a snare' (v.22).

2. That judgement took the form of assigning Judas to judicial hardening in his chosen course of sin. Literally, God gave him up. 'May their eyes be darkened so that they cannot see' (v.23).

3. Judas was placed under the unquenchable wrath of God with no possibility of mercy—a truth we've seen

already in Hebrews 6 and 10. 'Let your fierce anger overtake them' (v.24).

4. Judas went out into the night both literally and spiritually. 'May their place be deserted' (v.25). (The verse specifically cited in Acts 1:20.)

5. He plotted with others all that was to afflict the Lord in God's purposes. 'For they persecute those you wound and talk about the pain of those you hurt' (v.26).

6. He forfeited all possibility of salvation, becoming in Jesus' words a 'son of perdition'. 'Do not let them share in your salvation' (v.27).

7. He was thus, in common with all apostates, lost for ever. 'May they be blotted out of the book of life and not be listed with the righteous' (v.28).

What Peter saw in this Psalm was that before Pentecost could be experienced by this embryonic church of 120 disciples, God had to rid it of the faithless and unbelieving. The Psalm continually speaks in terms of the plural personal pronoun 'them' and 'they', for although it found its primary fulfilment in Judas, every generation of believers has seen Judas' apostasy repeated in their midst by men and women of Judas' ilk. And what was important for Peter and the rest to realize, as it is for us today, is that although Judas could at one time have been counted as 'one of their number' and even 'shared in this ministry', what Psalm 69 makes clear is that he had no share in the *salvation* which the Saviour purchased at so great a price. Whatever stumbling block and pain the apostasy of Judas was to prove to those 120 who witnessed his treachery firsthand, it was not, nor ever could be, the stumbling block it might have been had they entertained the possibility that a *saved person could be lost*.

Apostates have no 'share in your salvation'; they are 'blotted out of the book of life' and are not to 'be listed with the righteous' (Ps 69:27–28). Judas' actions were the actions of an unsaved man, and the facts which therefore emerged for their comfort from Psalm 69 can be summarized like this:

1. Judas' apostasy was predicted by God long before it happened.

2. His actions never took God by surprise.

3. They were the actions of a fake and a charlatan who had sneaked his way in among their number but never really belonged.

4. Those actions had ultimately served the purposes of God in saving men by the sufferings and death of his Son on the cross.

And so, in anticipation of the judgement when all pretenders and charlatans would be removed from the church for ever, God had removed Judas, who in total despair and tearful remorse had died the cursed death of one hung on a tree (Acts 1:18, Mt 27:5). It is interesting to note that this same Apostle Peter, who gained such insight into the death of Judas as he meditated upon Psalm 69, also wrote the words of 1 Peter 4:17–18,

> For it is time for judgment to begin with the family of God; and if it begins with us, what will the outcome be for those who *do not obey the gospel of God*? And, 'If it is hard for the righteous to be saved, what will become of the *ungodly and the sinner*?'

It must have been the source of some real consolation to Peter and the others to have realized that Judas could only have done what he did because in spite of all *appearances* to the contrary he was in fact one who did not 'obey the gospel of God' and was therefore to be ranked among 'the ungodly and the sinner'.

The contrast couldn't be more marked, for it was *Peter* who saw this. He himself, as we have seen, had denied the Lord. The difference was this: Peter's actions issued in repentance and change, Judas' actions issued only in remorse and then death. 2 Corinthians 7:8–10 highlights the vast contrast between these two reactions: 'Godly sorrow brings repentance that leads to salvation and leaves no regret, but worldly sorrow brings death' (v.10).

Judas is an example of what Paul here calls 'worldly sorrow'. Such sorrow feels badly about its sin, but confesses that sin not to God, but only to itself, in regretful re-runs of its shameful deeds. It may even make a person feel so badly that it leads him to commit suicide.

'Godly sorrow', by contrast, confesses to God and turns back to him no matter how deeply it has sunk in the mire of sin. It issues in a powerful return to God and a subsequent change of life.

> See what this godly sorrow has produced in you: what earnestness, what eagerness to clear yourselves, what indignation, what alarm, what longing, what concern, what readiness to see justice done. At every point you have proved yourselves to be innocent in this matter (v.11).

Judas remained, and remained to the end, a worldly man who died in 'worldly sorrow'. This, ultimately, is the explanation of his apostasy and should be comforting to all of God's people who have feared they could commit such an act. You could not.

By comparison and by contrast you *could* fall, as Peter did, into backsliding of the worst kind. But this always issues in 'godly sorrow' and real efforts to return and be restored, just as it did in the case of Peter. When that occurs, as it surely will, you will be reinstated to the place you so tragically forfeited by your disobedience and rebellion.

The backslider can lose the joy of salvation, but he cannot lose salvation itself. The examples of Judas and Peter, both present among the circle of Jesus' original disciples, make clear the vital distinctions we have sought to establish in this book as a whole. The fall of the apostate is permanent, that of the backslider is only temporary. The punishment of the apostate is eternal, that of the backslider is only temporal in that the apostate is abandoned by God for ever, but the backslider is chastened by God until he decides to return. The sin of the apostate is total, involving the complete renunciation of Christ and so leaving no room for repentance, forgiveness and change; whereas the sin of the backslider is partial, giving way one day to complete repentance and restoration under the full smile and favour of the Father he offended.

How long will the chastening of the backslider take before his restoration is accomplished? We do not know. But what we do know is this: God will stop at nothing to see the life he has planted within our hearts permeate the whole of our being and return back to him in such a way that it fully reflects his glory.

When that glory is masked and obscured through sin, Hebrews 12:1–12 tells us that because of his great love for his sons, God will chasten us in order to separate us from our sins and our sins from us. At those times the severity of God's hand can be agonizingly painful for us to experience. But it comes from the heart of One who is bent on our perfection (Heb 12: 4–11), and comes also as an unmistakable proof of his love. It is not us God hates, but our sin.

Listen to these words from a poem by Dale Stone entitled 'The Shaping of a Disciple'.

> When God wants to drill a man
> And thrill a man, and skill a man,
> When God wants to mould a man
> To play for Him the noblest part,
> When He yearns with all His heart
> To build so great and bold a man
> That all the world shall be amazed,
> Then watch God's methods, watch His ways!
> How He ruthlessly perfects
> Whom He royally elects;
> How He hammers him and hurts him,
> And with mighty blows converts him,
> Making shapes and forms, which only

God Himself can understand,
Even while his man is crying,
Lifting a beseeching hand . . .
Yet God bends but never breaks
When man's good He undertakes;
When He uses whom He chooses,
And with every purpose fuses
Man to act and act to Man,
As it was when He began;
When God tries His splendour out,
Man will know what He's about![20]

Let's be clear about this: disciples will be disciplined! And never more so than when they are in a state of backsliding. That's what makes such a condition the most miserable time of our lives. But remember, 'No discipline seems pleasant at the time, but painful. Later on, however, it produces a harvest of righteousness and peace for those who have been trained by it' (Heb 12:11).

If we are sure that the apostate will be lost through his own folly, we are doubly sure that the backslider will be restored through God's grace. How do we know? We have God's word on it. That is enough. Just wait and see.

12

Simon Magus—Spiritual Power: Real and Counterfeit

Have you ever awoken in total surprise to find yourself warmly cocooned under your quilt when, only moments before, you were flying alone and unaided high over fields and rivers and gliding gracefully through the sunlit breezy air currents of some imaginary flightpath? Of course, the flight was the dream, and the blankets the reality. How disappointing to be brought back to earth in this way, and to realize that you do not possess the abilities of unassisted flight nor, so far as you are aware, ever will.

Although we can learn to live with the fact that we cannot fly, there are thousands of men, women and young people who nurse a growing discontentment that human powers seem curtailed like this in so many ways. They move about with a constant sense of disappointment akin to the feelings I've just described. They wish it were possible to do more, to move out in supernatural ways, to escape from the confines in which our normal expectations bind us. Such people believe that great powers lie dormant in every one of us, and that extraordinary abilities may be awakened, handicaps and limitations removed, and horizons of present prospects considerably widened, *if only we knew how*.

The truth is, God has always intended that ordinary

men and women should move in extraordinary ways. He planned for each of us to be indwelt by and alive to the flow of his Holy Spirit and therefore open to the possibility of being a people who move in the powers of two worlds. We can be creatures of earth and heaven, such that we are both naturally supernatural and supernaturally natural at the same time. These abilities have been lost through sin but are restored in Christ. People once characterized by rebellion and so justly evicted from the divine Presence (Gen 3) may be restored and forgiven through the pardon purchased so expensively by the blood of God's Son. Made one with Christ as members of his body upon earth, the Father then equips us to minister his supernatural power once again in this needy world which cries out for the dominion of the power of God's kingdom ministered through the means of kingdom people.

Of course, the *legitimate* way to true spiritual power is rejected by others who nevertheless still long for the recovery of the powers and abilities which they are convinced we have lost. Such people are open to great deception as they seek spiritual power along pathways prohibited in God's word (Deut 18:9–13). Refusing the voice of God speaking in his word, they follow the beguiling deceivers who promise much but give little. Walk into any average well-stocked bookshop and scan the shelves headed 'Religion' or 'Philosophy'. You will perhaps see a tiny selection of Christian paperbacks, but the overwhelming proportion of titles on display will be an extensive array dealing with Zen, Eastern Mysticism, Fortune-telling, Parapsychology, Tarot and the so-called New Age techniques for the advancement of personal power and the attainment of self-fulfilment.

Similarly, to observe the ratings of popular entertainment videos or the guest line-up for television chat shows is at the same time to notice the enormous popularity of material or personalities which deal with the occult, satanic or spirit-world of mediums and their séances.

People want power but they do not want it God's way.

In Acts 8 we read something of the curious history of a man who made a remarkable brush with Christianity, even to the point of being baptized and admitted to the membership of the church, yet who later came under the severest censure of the Apostle Peter and in point of fact proved to be a notorious apostate from the ranks of Christian people. His name was Simon Magus.

> Now for some time a man named Simon had practised sorcery in the city and amazed all the people of Samaria. He boasted that he was someone great, and all the people, both high and low, gave him their attention and exclaimed, 'This man is the divine power known as the Great Power'. They followed him because he had amazed them for a long time with his magic. But when they believed Philip as he preached the good news of the kingdom of God and the name of Jesus Christ, they were baptised, both men and women. Simon himself believed and was baptised. And he followed Philip everywhere, astonished by the great signs and miracles he saw.
>
> When the apostles in Jerusalem heard that Samaria had accepted the word of God, they sent Peter and John to them. When they arrived, they prayed for them that they might receive the Holy Spirit, because the Holy Spirit had not yet come upon any of them; they had simply been baptised into the name of the Lord Jesus. Then Peter and John placed their hands on them, and they received the Holy Spirit.
>
> When Simon saw that the Spirit was given at the laying on of the apostles' hands, he offered them money and said, 'Give me also this ability so that everyone on whom I lay my hands may receive the Holy Spirit.'
>
> Peter answered: 'May your money perish with you, because you thought you could buy the gift of God with money! You have no part or share in this ministry, because your heart is not right before God. Repent of this wickedness and pray to the Lord. Perhaps he will forgive you for having such a thought in your heart. For I see that you are full of bitterness and captive to sin.'
>
> Then Simon answered, 'Pray to the Lord for me so that nothing you have said may happen to me' (Acts 8:9–24).

Why do people first become curious about and then actually seek involvement in the forbidden realms of occult forces? Simon Magus illustrates the answer to that question forcefully. Simon Magus had wanted *power*: 'A man named Simon had practised sorcery in the city and amazed all the people of Samaria' (v.9). He had actually done extraordinary things before the careful eyes of many witnesses. Don't be mistaken, the devil is prepared to give power—working, spiritual power—to those foolish enough to succumb to his enticements. Satan promises to impart to us power over the natural world, over future circumstances and over other people.

This is why experimentation in telepathy, levitation techniques, hypnosis, palmistry, water divining, ouija, magic charms and curses can often meet with signal results which baffle even the practitioner. Satan lures his gullible victims into the damning webs of counterfeit spiritual power. Simon Magus had used the first-century equivalent of some of these techniques, and drawing upon demonic influence had moved in the impressive demonstration of occult power which he so eagerly pursued.

Furthermore, in common with so many, he had found that such displays had brought him *fame and popularity*. He boasted that he was someone great and the people both high and low gave him their attention and exclaimed, 'This man is the divine power known as the Great Power.' They followed him because he had amazed them for a long time with his magic. Perhaps it is because such people feel acutely the present insignificance of their lives that they will pay any price in order to elevate their humdrum existence to the supposedly higher planes of adventure, excitement and even a certain degree of notoriety. They clamour for praise, adoration and the wonderment of gaping mouths or bulging eyes as their supernatural deeds stir the curiosity of friends and, perhaps, may ultimately even win the adulation of the masses. Of course, they would protest that their 'healings' or 'powers' exist only to *serve* their fellow human beings, and, in feigned humility, will loudly protest any hint of criticism along lines exposing the true nature of their motives. Well, we'd hardly expect them to say, 'Yes, we've come to bleed you white and fleece the very skin from your backs!'

Usually, under the guise of benevolence, such practitioners are eager for the money of the credulous and the gullible. They are selfish and egotistical. Like Simon Magus they boast that they are 'someone great' and they revel in the popular interpretations as to the source of their power, 'This man is the divine power known as the Great Power.'

Satan is an unrepentant egotist. It follows that his ambassadors and emissaries will be too. How sad, then, that even among genuinely-gifted ministers and servants of Christ, this kind of pride can creep in. The healing evangelist indulges in false and unrealistic claims about what has been achieved through his ministry. The itinerant preacher, moving in signs and wonders, is under such pressure to produce results that the reports of God's blessing must be published for his eager circle of followers, even if they have to be invented. And so like their satanic counterparts, such ministries are often accompanied by a flamboyant style in either dress or manner, arrogant and scathing criticism of others, persistent and intrusive appeals for money, and a positive revelling in the attention of others, particularly if that favourable interest is being shown by the media. God's power *is* available to his people, but in our pursuit of it (1 Cor 14:1) we must shun all display of self. The glory is to go to him and not to us. Therein lies the path of safety.

As we watch Simon Magus pursue Christian things we must remember the motivation of his heart which is revealed here. So many people, as we have seen, become caught up in the church and in spiritual things, often for less than the best motives. Such people, unless their motivation changes, will prove prime candidates for a fall, sitting targets for Satan's allurements away from the Lord.

The spiritual power available to God's people, with all its attendant effects and results, could not stand in starker contrast to all this. It is the power to *serve*, and it is utterly self-effacing. When God touches a believing man or woman with the power of his Spirit it is with two main ends in mind.

First, *to minister to others*. In these same verses, how lovely it is to watch the evangelist Philip go to work: 'With shrieks, evil spirits came out of many, and many paralytics and cripples were healed. So there was great joy in that city' (Acts 8:7–8). His motivation was to bring wholeness and healing into the lives of others, to undo the doleful effects of sin and of Satan in the lives of their pathetic victims. He aimed to speak the word that would cause faith to be born within them. He desired to pray and convey God's blessings upon them. In true spirituality, it's never the case that we chase after power for power's sake, nor even power for our own sake, but rather power for the sake of others. It is power to serve the needs of others.

Secondly, it is power *to bring glory to Jesus Christ*. Again, look at Philip: 'He preached the good news of the kingdom of God and the name of Jesus Christ' (v.12). Here is the Christian's great ambition in pursuing spiritual gifts and making himself available for God to use in displays of divine power. It is not to climb some ecclesiastical ladder or to be seen coast to coast on prime-time television, but rather to enhance in the eyes of men, the glory, living reality and truth of Jesus Christ. 'Whatever you do, do it all for the glory of God' (1 Cor 10:31). 'To him be the glory for ever! Amen' (Rom 11:36).

Notice also the deliberate diversion of glory *from* himself *to* Jesus Christ which is recorded of Peter: 'If we are being called to account today for an act of kindness shown to a cripple and are asked how he was healed, then know this . . . It is by the name of Jesus Christ of

Nazareth' (Acts 4:9–10). If we are privileged to see people saved, healed or delivered through our ministry towards them, then uppermost in our minds must be this question, a question designed to jolt us into the proper perspective on these issues: 'Who did it?' And the unhesitating conviction of every believing heart is to answer unequivocally, 'Why Jesus, of course!' That being so, he should get all the glory. 'For we do not preach ourselves, but Jesus Christ as Lord, and ourselves as your servants for Jesus' sake' (2 Cor 4:5).

What emerges here in the narrative is that Simon Magus never really abandoned his false and carnal motivation in the seeking of spiritual power.

When Philip the evangelist, and later Peter the Apostle, came to preach and minister in Samaria, Simon saw greater displays of wonder-working energy than he had ever seen in his life. He made a false profession of faith, although the language used would seem at first glance to indicate otherwise: 'Simon himself believed and was baptised' (v.13). The alarm bells begin to sound, however, when Luke tells us, 'And he followed Philip everywhere, astonished by the great signs and miracles he saw' (v.13).

As we discovered in the parable of the sower, Jesus taught that there is a temporary faith which upon hearing the word may 'receive it with joy' but 'since they have no root, they last only a short time' (Mk 4:16–17). Such people respond keenly and enthusiastically at first, perhaps profoundly impressed by the demonstrations they have seen, especially if signs and wonders have accompanied the preaching of the gospel. But there has been no surrender of the will, no submission of the mind, no radical recreation of the spirit in true regeneration, and therefore no actual yielding to Christ.

The tell-tale signs of false conversion are clearly seen in Simon. As we have seen already, he could more accurately be described as a follower of the Lord's *servants* than a follower of the *Lord* himself: 'He followed Philip everywhere' (v.13). In common with others displaying an equally false conversion, there is an attachment to Christ's men rather than to Christ himself. This may happen in a number of ways—attracted to a good-looking fellow or girl in the church; the pull of an impressive preacher or pulpit personality. Still others come under the influence of a loyal personal friend or popular public figure who believes in the Lord and whom they secretly want to emulate. But to follow men when there is no heart attachment to Christ is a dangerous activity because it frequently entails a look-alike type of conversion and falls short of the real thing.

Simon Magus appears to have been drawn more by spectacle than God's holiness. He was 'astonished by the great signs and miracles he saw'. The faith provoked by miracles may not be the faith which unites a person to Christ. Simon is here seen excitedly pursuing Philip's miraculous ministry, and later indulging in unabashed appreciation of Peter's power to convey the Spirit (vv.18–19), but the main purpose and thrust of this kingdom power in spectacular display completely escaped him. Simon did not know that the Holy Spirit has come not merely to heal bodies but to make our spirits holy, cleanse our lives, and reorientate the whole course of our destinies. He was content just to marvel at the spectacular effects which he saw and to think of it all simply as a superior brand of sorcery, a brand also available to him if only *he knew how* it might be obtained.

Most disturbing of all, the evidence indicates that he continued to view religion, even the religion of Christ, as a money-making racket and not as a gracious reality.

'When Simon saw that the Spirit was given at the laying on of the apostles' hands, he offered them money and said, "Give me also this ability so that everyone on whom I lay my hands may receive the Holy Spirit."' Peter the Apostle had come to assess Philip's work. He discovered great numbers of Samaritans who had been regenerated and professed genuine faith in Christ by being baptised. Each of these new converts needed to be brought swiftly into their New Testament birthright of receiving the Holy Spirit in fullness and in power.

Peter had preached this privilege on the Day of Pentecost, indicating that the exceptional experience of some Old Testament saints (e.g. prophets, priests, judges and kings) had become the normal inheritance for all God's people since Jesus' ascension to the right hand of God (Acts 2:33, 38–39). The Holy Spirit is now willing, at Christ's orders, to 'come upon' all believers in order to endue them with power for witness (Acts 1:8) and service in the body of Christ (1 Cor 12:13). Sometimes the Spirit's enduement in this way (called variously in the New Testament 'being baptised' or 'being filled' with the Spirit) is accompanied by spectacular and visible effects. The new believers may burst forth in ecstatic joy, and praise God in languages previously unknown to them (Acts 2:1 ff; 10:46; 19:6) and this may have been what happened to the Samaritans here in Acts 8. At any rate, as Peter prayed and laid hands upon them and as they were anointed with the Spirit so that he 'came upon them' (see Acts 8:15–16), something visible, wonderful and inexplicable at a natural level began to happen to them.

Simon saw what Philip and Peter could do, and coveted the power to achieve those same results for himself. He offered to pay Peter a sum of money for the 'secret', rather like a member of the Magic Circle might make a financial deal with a colleague, for the details of an impressive new stunt or spectacular illusion.

The truth about all apostates is that they never finally surrender the conviction they secretly nurse that, at base, all religion is really a racket designed for one's own personal advancement or the advancement of others as corrupt as oneself. We saw it in the materialism and covetousness of Judas. The same spirit manifests itself in Simon Magus. It has given rise to the sin known as

'Simony' which has plagued the Christian church ever since. Simon thought that ecclesiastical position and power could be bought with the right sum, through bribery and 'backhanders'. He therefore attempted to 'grease the palm' of the Apostle Peter himself.

No wonder Peter's response is so vigorous and powerful. He says in verse 20, 'May your money perish with you, because you thought you could buy the gift of God with money.' We're not exaggerating the force of these words if we translate them, 'To hell with you and your money!' With true Spirit-given discernment and a total refusal to compromise, Peter resolutely dismissed the thought for ever, that God's grace or power could be bought with a few jangling coins or crumpled paper notes, as if the gospel was some kind of slot machine which dispensed blessings like chocolate bars or cigarettes to any depositor with the right change and the correct sum of money.

It was Peter's verdict that Simon had 'no part or share in this ministry' and that his heart was 'not right before God' (v.21). With that same discernment exercised in the case of Ananias and Sapphira, Peter was enabled to see beyond Simon Magus' profession of faith into a heart still 'full of bitterness and captive to sin' (v.23). And Peter could only repeat the call which Simon Magus had previously heard from evangelist Philip, 'Repent of this wickedness and pray to the Lord. Perhaps he will forgive you for having such a thought in your heart' (v.22).

Yet even in the face of such powerful and direct diagnosis, delivered with such faithfulness and integrity, Simon displays the qualities of a man seeking only a quick escape from his punishment and not a radical conversion from his sin. Peter has told him in effect, 'You are not yet converted. You are still in slavery to sin; your heart is full of pollution; your life is bent upon wickedness. You do not qualify in any way to be a servant or minister of Christ in your present condition.' What was Simon's response? 'Pray to the Lord for me so that nothing you have said may happen to me' (v.24). Here is a man who fears the punishment of sin, but does not fear its enslaving condition. He can ask others to pray for him, but he will not pray for himself. He wanted only an easy escape, not a radical change; a free ride, but not a full pardon and total renewal of his nature. He sought the security of a divine insurance policy, but didn't realize that the premiums would involve from the beginning the complete surrender of his life. Here is another example of remorse without repentance. A remorse motivated only by self-interest, cowardice and fear.

Extra-biblical sources tell us that Simon Magus went on to become a bitter opponent of the apostles in particular and of Christ's church in general, a notorious heretic, and a pioneer of a particularly insidious example of false teaching which was later to cause great trouble in the church—the error of Gnosticism. The truth we saw in Hebrews 6 and 10 was borne out in the subsequent career of the apostate, Simon Magus. Very few people become more rabid opponents of Christ or more destructive of the faith than those who have had the experience of 'once being enlightened' and of tasting 'the goodness of the word of God and the powers of the coming age'. Their knowledge fuels the fires of their resentment and sharpens the edge of their cutting hostility towards Christ and his people.

The preaching and practice of the apostles in the early church, as recorded both here in Acts 8 and elsewhere, would indicate that true conversion and a growing faith of the kind Peter preached (for example, in Acts 2:38–42) involves the coming together of four ingredients in the lives of those who eventually give a proper hearing to the preaching of the gospel, and the presentation of Christ as the crucified, resurrected and ascended Lord. Here are those four responses, sometimes dubbed 'The Peter Package'.

Repentance—the admission that I've been wrong, the

cessation of my rebellion and the abandonment of my sin with no reservations and no conditions on my part whatsoever.

Faith—complete persuasion of what Christ has done for me, and total surrender to him as Lord.

These first two ingredients are the essentials of coming into salvation. Between these and the next lies the watershed. Healthy Christianity and progress in the truth requires that one has confessed one's faith in the God-appointed manner of water baptism, and been empowered for service by the God-ordained way of Spirit baptism.

Baptism in water—the burning of bridges in a public identification with Christ and his people by total immersion in water; an act performed in the name of the Father, the Son and the Holy Spirit and followed by the joining of his church. ('And about three thousand were *added to their number* that day', Acts 2:41.)

Baptism in the Spirit—a conscious reception of the Spirit's anointing with power to equip me for witness and service, and to bring me into the place where I can function properly in the church which is Christ's body, and flow in his gifts for the blessing of my fellow believers and effective outreach into the world.

Simon Magus never repented of the sinful routes to spiritual power which he had previously pursued, nor of the occult practices in which he had once freely indulged. He never came to the point where his life was cast unconditionally upon Jesus as Saviour and Lord. Consequently, his belief was inadequate and only temporary, his baptism in water a sham, and his baptism in the Spirit non-existent. He was still 'full of bitterness and captive to sin' (v.23).

Simon Magus is another terrifying example in Scripture of a man who came so near to the truth and yet at the same time stood aloof from it: *so near and yet so far*. He was a man who ultimately perished along with his money, his magic and his manipulation of God's truth.

This is the ugly sin of apostasy, and it is in order that you may avoid such a sin that this book has been written.

We have now completed our representative selection of vivid case studies from Scripture. These have helped to throw light on the nagging questions springing from the difficult passages in Hebrews 6 and 10, which have vexed us from the beginning of our study.

We are now going to draw the threads of all this teaching together in what, I believe, is a very practical and salutary concluding chapter based on how the writer to the Hebrews handles this disturbing pastoral problem. This chapter is designed to help those who know someone who is already on the slippery slope I've described. The epilogue is for those who have seen *themselves* described in the preceding chapters and are concerned to do something about it.

Conclusion

13

A Terrible Danger and Its God-Given Remedy

We return to the place at which we began. We are going to conclude with the unfolding of a very important passage in the epistle to the Hebrews. In this book we have surveyed some of the frightening steps on the descent towards that very slippery slope, which in turn plummets into the bottomless chasm of apostasy. We have spent some time in the unsavoury company of an unholy family of sins peculiar to the lives of professing believers, and whose portrait is given to us in the pages of Holy Scripture. Each member of that family turned out to be more debased and hardened than the one which came before. We have been sobered and shaken by the examples of Peter and Gehazi, Hymenaeus and Alexander, Ananias and Sapphira, Judas and Simon Magus. And we have searched into their conduct as they modelled, before our eyes, sins serious enough to frighten the wits out of us. They may be conveniently summarized under four headings:

1. The 'overtaken' saint or backslider (Gal 6:1)

He is drifting from the Lord, but not disqualified from service, and he may be completely restored to a healthy life with the Lord if the right measures are quickly taken to see him brought back both to God and to his people.

2. The reject or castaway (1 Cor 9:27)

This person, through some serious fall, has marred his usefulness and perhaps ended his ministry for ever. There are some sins, the consequences of which cannot be undone in this life, and which may disqualify us from our ministry, at least the ministry we were engaged in before that momentous fall.

3. The shipwreck (1 Tim 1:19–20)

This person, on the verge of apostasy, has come so near to abandoning the faith that the severe chastening of God has fallen upon him. He may even die, if such drastic discipline becomes a necessity, in order to save him from total ruin.

4. The apostate (Heb 6, 10; Jude 12–13; 2 Pet 2:21–23)

He may well have received an experience of a very high order as to the truth and beauty of Christianity, but he later rejects and abandons it all in wilful obstinacy and with full knowledge of the consequences of his action. For such a person there is no possibility whatsoever of recovery and restoration.

The above list shows an evident progression. That's why the condition we commonly call 'backsliding' is so serious. It is the start of the slippery slope which eventually leads to apostasy and complete abandonment of the faith. This is why the writer to the Hebrews addresses the assembled congregations of his readers with this very important word of timely exhortation:

> See to it, brothers, that none of you has a sinful, unbelieving heart that turns away from the living God. But encourage one another daily, as long as it is called Today, so that none of you may be hardened by sin's deceitfulness (Heb 3:12–13).

It was the burden of the writer's heart that his readers should realize that the Christian faith is not something a person can *take* and then *leave, keep to* for a while and then *quit* simply as the mood suits him. Even in the face of obstacles, trials and the severest temptations, we must persevere in the faith at all costs. 'We have come to share in Christ *if we hold firmly till the end* the confidence we had at first' (Heb 3:14, my italics). The whole epistle to the Hebrews is an echo of the emphasis we find throughout Scripture upon perseverence through trial. Typical of this vital emphasis are those words describing Paul's ministry in Acts 14:21–22:

> They preached the good news in that city and won a large number of disciples. Then they returned to Lystra, Iconium and Antioch, strengthening the disciples and encouraging them to remain true to the faith. 'We must go through many hardships to enter the kingdom of God,' they said.

The Hebrew Christians were, in many cases, in danger of giving up. In the face of hostility and false teaching they had begun to ask such serious questions as, 'Why has God allowed me to go through this?' and, 'Do I really believe what I say I believed?' They were drifting dangerously into defeat, despair and despondency.

It's quite safe to depart from gods which are *dead*. If you throw away your Zodiac signs or your rabbit's foot, no harm could ever come to you. But their danger was one of departing from the *living* God. That is the road to death. Hence the severe warnings in this epistle which we have already examined.

The danger is described in Hebrews 3 as *becoming hardened*. As summer gives way to autumn, and that season in turn yields to the bitter cold of winter, have you ever watched a lake or pond freezing over in those sub-zero temperatures? Probably not, because the process takes quite some time. It is a gradual development beginning almost imperceptibly yet, in freezing conditions, continuing until the surface is so thickly encrusted with ice that it will bear the weight of many men.

Backsliding is always a slow but sure business too. As

with the pond, it begins with a loss of heat internally. A certain over-confidence in oneself or presumptuousness and pride gives way to the neglect of such basics as prayer, Bible reading and fellowship. In time, like Samson who 'did not know that the Lord had left him' (Judg 16:20), the backslider hardly notices that God's felt presence has been absent for so long. Inevitably the Christian life loses its zest and attraction, while at the same time sin doesn't seem half so bad as he'd once been led to believe. His conscience becomes calloused and desensitized, the unthinkable becomes thinkable, the thinkable becomes possible, the possible becomes actual. Very soon he is frequenting the company of old friends, back at the old haunts, and sins once repented of are not only tolerated but willingly indulged.

Heat hardens clay and melts wax. It is the nature of the two substances which determines the result. In the same way testings and trials expose the condition of our hearts. As we face them they either melt and tenderize our sensitivity towards God and his will, or become occasions of our yielding to temptation and beginning the process of hardening our hearts. Once sin is entertained it inevitably hardens us. All sin has the potential to do this in the life of each of us. This hardening is reflected in the boredom and indifference with which the Christian life is approached. Preaching is irrelevant, worship meaningless, and Christian company a drag.

How does this dangerous condition come about? Hebrews 3:13 says that it is through *sin's deceitfulness* 'so that none of you may be hardened by sin's deceitfulness'. We are here clued in to the nature of sin's approach. It is always camouflaged and disguised. It neither paints itself accurately in its true colours as it presents itself to us, nor does it spell out in detail the end results of embracing it. The serpent hides his fangs well and may even present himself to us in the form of a harmless dove. Sin, by nature, is deceptive. Otherwise who would submit to its wicked designs?

In Hebrews 10:25–26 the writer clearly implies that much of the dangerous drifting indulged in by his readers went hand in hand with irregularity in meeting with their fellow believers. He says, 'Let us not give up meeting together, as some are in the habit of doing.' No doubt the absentees justified all this in their own minds as perfectly reasonable behaviour. 'It's the weather . . . my bad back means I can't sit for long . . . I watch the service on the TV . . . I find more than one sermon a week too hard to take in . . .' I once had a backslidden Christian explain to me his five-year absence from the church fellowship in this way, 'I meet with Christians on the street!' By which he meant that he bumped in to them from time to time and had some conversation with them, and that was surely enough! How deceitful sin is!

The deceits of sin take many forms and many disguises. The sin might be sexual, called in Ephesians 4:22 'deceitful desires'. Such sins are often justified by what Ephesians 5:6 calls 'empty words': 'How can it be wrong if we love each other?' 'If it feels good it must be good.' 'Times have changed: the Bible was written then, but this is now.' 'God understands—I have a weakness in this area.'

The sin may be the lure of material riches, called in Matthew 13:22 'the deceitfulness of wealth', which has led the drifting church member to say, 'I need all of this overtime; we've got so many financial commitments to the family,' or, 'We should turn the corner next year, then I can think about putting God first.'

It may be the enticing attraction of false teaching called in Colossians 2:8 'hollow and deceptive philosophy' which presents itself as abreast with the findings and researches of modern scholarship and able to look down scathingly upon 'narrow and obscurantist' Christian belief.

The young Christian begins going out with an unbeliever unsympathetic to her faith. At first it was only a casual friendship, then a date or two, and now a close bond in which they see one another most evenings of the week and also at weekends. The Bible may say, 'Do not be yoked together with unbelievers. For what do righteousness and wickedness have in common? Or what fellowship can light have with darkness?' (2 Cor 6:14), but in her case God made an exception. After all, she's looking for an opportunity to witness to him and bring him to church. How would he hear the gospel if she just ignored him? I've not only seen such girls seduced into sexual sin while working in their private 'mission field', but some have gone on to marry the man and have then lived for years with the desperate hope that their unsaved husband would come to embrace the faith of his wife which he had long since demonstrated he had no interest in whatsoever.

Sin never comes to us in honesty, openness and completely above-board. It doesn't portray accurately to its victims the loss of joy, erosion of peace, shame to Christ, and eventual shipwreck it will bring into their lives. No, it presents to us only the apparent *advantages* of following its enticements. We'll gain valuable experience, broaden our minds, extend our usefulness, know a bit more about life, or get a kick out of life. How true! But with this qualification: the kick will be to the head, and the ensuing wound may be fatal. And so embracing this *deceiver* we become in turn *deceived*. We cannot see what misery we're plunging ourselves into, what grief we bring to the Spirit of God, what shame to the Lord Jesus Christ, what a stumbling-block we are to the church, and what a scandal we are to those unbelievers who, unknown to us, have watched our faithless actions. Nor do we catch even a glimpse of the rejoicing in hell, the weeping among the angels, and the deep sorrow felt by those who love us most. We are being 'hardened through the deceitfulness of sin'.

The wonderful remedy God proposes for this condition is given to us in verse 13, 'But encourage one another daily, as long as it is called Today.' The remedy is that

Christian people *encourage* one another, not, please note, 'commiserate' with one another by fuelling each other's resentment and complaints. The passage Hebrews 3:7–11, in the immediate context, harks back to the wanderings of Israel when a whole generation perished in the wilderness and failed to enter God's rest. If you've read Exodus and Numbers you'll know that one of the chief sins of that period was the sin of complaining. In their rebellion they grumbled against God, against his appointed leaders Moses and Aaron, against the route they were taking and the conditions they met with on the way. 'Why no water? Where's the food? I'm sick of this Manna! We're being misled! Who do you leaders think you are?' A negative critical mood overtook them and God consigned them to what Luis Palau called 'forty years of desert vagrancy' and, of course, also to eventual death.

Much of the restlessness, discontentment, lack of peace, fruitlessness and negativism prevalent in Christian circles today is fuelled by our inveterate weakness for negative criticism and complaint. When someone is backsliding the most many of us do is give a sympathetic ear to their complaints, and perhaps in the process pass on more grist for their mill as they deepen their resentment towards the church and its people.

What is it to '*encourage* one another'? It means more than saying: 'Stop complaining!' and pointing out the good things God has done for us.

In the context of this verse the word means '*shout out* to one another' (from the verb *parakaleō*, to call to, to exhort, to urge, to entreat, admonish or beseech). If you saw a blind man with a white cane tapping his way to the edge of the pavement of a busy high street, and then saw him move to step out under the wheels of the speeding traffic, what would you do? You would *shout out to him*, 'Stop! You'll be killed! Don't do it! Halt!' Well, that's what God says we are to do with the backslider. God works by means, and the means God has ordained to pull these dangerous drifters up in their tracks is the faithful speaking of their fellow Christians. But it must be with words spoken into the *right* ears.

So often in these situations we talk to each other ('Have you heard about Steve? Yes, he's back with that gang from the other side of town again'), and we may even talk to the Lord ('I think we should pray for Steve, he really needs our prayers at this time'), but often the last person we speak to is the *backslider* himself ('I think we should just ignore Steve for the time being, that should bring him to his senses').

God's word to us is as plain as it is simple. He says, in effect, 'When you see the ice forming, don't wait until it is so thick you couldn't penetrate it with a sledge hammer. Wade into that situation while you can; shout out to him; speak into his life; break up the chilly ice of his dangerous drifting while it's still only in its early stages.'

We are to call a halt to their despondency, misery and complaints. Taking as our model the epistle to the Hebrews itself, we are to teach, encourage, urge on and warn seriously of the consequences of their backsliding should it continue unhalted.

Since the writer is not specific as to whose responsibility this is, we must conclude that it is a word for *all* of us. It is intended for the elders of the church certainly, but it also applies to husbands and their wives, to parents and their children, to you and your friends. If you are the first to see the condition, then yours is the first responsibility to act and to do something about it. 'Brothers, if someone is caught in a sin, you who are spiritual should restore him gently . . . carry each other's burdens, and in this way you will fulfil the law of Christ' (Gal 6:1–2). Here is a loving desperation to stop the backslider before things deteriorate any further. Such desperation will mean risking personal insult and angry retaliation from the one he exhorts. Be encouraged, God will give you the words to say, and if all else fails then simply try tears! Few things are more effective in melting down cold, hardened hearts, than the hot, salty tears of friends who love them.

What these people most need to know is that they are loved. What we most need to realize is that sometimes love must be tough. Love doesn't consider its own welfare, but the welfare of others. So when we're tempted to excuse our inaction with such objections as, 'But what if they ignore me, or don't like what I have to say?', love answers with insistence and with urgency, 'You must defy their wrath and risk their ire if you are to see them restored.'

The writer says, 'Encourage one another *daily*.' This implies that this is a task in which we will have to engage ourselves quite frequently as we interact with one another (because sin is always deceiving somebody in the fellowship). It also implies persistence because some of sin's deceits will not yield to our efforts instantly. It also urges us to consistency (not giving up at the first hurdle). It may be that just one word will not be enough to restore the backslider. When Peter denied the Lord three times, Jesus was later to see him retrace those steps with the three-fold question, 'Do you truly love me? Do you truly love me? Do you love me?' (Jn 21:15–17). Surely the second and third questions were not superfluous. There will hardly be a week that goes by when this kind of exhortation will not be necessary. It will be a perpetual ministry in the church until Jesus returns. Why? Because sin is always going about its deceitful work, and people are always falling victim to it. Many potential disasters could be halted, and some precious lives saved, if we all took seriously the counsel of this verse in our relationships and interactions with one another.

As if that were not enough, the writer adds, 'Do it *today*,' or in his own words, 'As long as it is called Today,' for he wishes us to know that there is some *urgency* about this duty. If the opportunity to speak to that person is before us right now, then we must not let it slip, or tomorrow may be too late. But be encouraged as you go about this work, for this word 'today' also implies that God is eager to show mercy immediately; the backslider is not going to be put on probation for two years; he can be restored *today*.

God really has ensured us success in this task, not only in the words already quoted from Galatians 6:1–2, 'You who are spiritual should restore him gently,' but also in other passages such as, 'Whoever turns a sinner away from his error will save him from death and cover over a multitude of sins,' and, 'Be merciful to those who doubt; snatch others from the fire and save them; to others show mercy, mixed with fear' (Jas 5:20; Jude 22–23).

Do you know someone in danger of committing the sins described in this book? Someone who is drifting away from their faith and who has already embarked upon the slippery slope that leads from backsliding to apostasy and ultimately to a departure from the living God which is both final and for ever? Then do not delay. Go to them; say something and *say it today*.

14
The Lost Son Goes Home

I hate losing things—don't you? Especially if they are valuable. Yet value is hard to measure. How valuable are you? One chemist calculated the worth of a human being in terms of his constituent chemicals. Enough iron to make a few two-inch nails, enough lime to whitewash one chicken coop, enough phosphorous to tip half a dozen matches, enough sulphur to rid one dog of fleas, and so on. He came up with a grand total of around £1.17. More recently in 1978, Adam Starchild of the Minerva Consulting Group made some similar calculations by adding up the value of human biochemicals present in the body and checking his prices from specialist chemical company catalogues. Such substances as haemoglobin ($2.95 a gram) and the female hormone prolactin ($17,500,000 a gram) were introduced into these new calculations. The value of a single human being worked out at something like $6,000,000! Quite an advance on £1.17!

But people cannot be measured in such terms. People matter more than things. This is the thrust of probably the most well known of all the parables which Jesus told.

In Luke 15, Jesus tells three moving and memorable stories to illustrate how valuable you are to God and how pained and anxious for your recovery the Father is when you become lost. The Lord literally aches for your recovery. In the first story a man lost 1% of his sheep. In the second, a woman lost 10% of her coins (a valuable dowry worn as part of the headress on a young maiden's wedding day). And finally, in the third, he told of a father who lost 100% of his sons—one of those two boys knew that he was lost, and the other, the older brother, never came to that realization.

The most famous of the two lost sons, the younger brother, is so like the backslider. What the backslider needs to recover (if he ever really knew it at all) is a sense of the Father's love, and of how eagerly the Father awaits his return. If this book has revealed that your present condition is far removed from your former joy and enthusiasm, then I would appeal to you to come back home to where you really belong. In these parables Jesus is telling us that people matter more than animals or things. The movement is from sheep to coins to sons. There can't be any debate as to which mattered most. Losing people is the greatest pain any of us can experience, especially when we love and treasure them. How much more if the lost ones are your own children. Jesus wants us to see the backslider's position from his Father's viewpoint. Jesus is telling us that the Father's heart aches for the return of his lost sons and daughters, whether they are unsaved or simply backslidden.

I recently read a fascinating and moving newspaper report which concerned a lady in America, Mrs Wilma Henessy, who discovered that she had brought the wrong baby home from hospital some forty-eight years previously. The discovery was made when her forty-eight-year-old 'substitute' son brought home a novelty ashtray featuring his bare footprint. For fun they decided to compare this print with the print of that same son taken in hospital minutes after his birth. The prints were completely different. The dreadful truth began to dawn upon her. Since that spell in hospital at the time of his birth, she had never seen her real son and had no idea what he looked like or what had happened to him.

Thus began her search to find the son who was lost. Her reported words were very moving: 'I've not got long left . . . I just want to see my real son before I'm gone.' But though her real son is lost, the pain is all on one side. Presumably the son to whom she actually gave birth has no idea that he is lost.

It is like this with backsliding. If you are backslidden, do you know that you are lost to your Father God? In this story, Jesus not only wants you to see how God feels about that, he also wants you to see yourself as you really are. It could be like looking into a mirror after a dreadful accident and asking, 'Is that really me?' Gradually the truth needs to dawn upon you that it really is you! Yes, you are the one Jesus described in the story. Let's look at the portrait Jesus gives us of the boy who ran away from home.

This boy had left his father's *heart*. His words 'Father, give me my share of the estate' (Lk 15:12) contain more pain than is evident on the surface. The son knew he only inherited upon his father's death. In speeding forward the effects of that day in advance, the son was saying in these few words: 'I wish you were already dead, Father. I can't be comfortable around you. I resent your authority over me. I find your words, your requests, your presence and your wishes an irritating intrusion into my life. I want out, and I want what's mine right now. I can't kill you, I know, but I wish you were dead. Give me my share of the inheritance now.' You can't murder God, but you can wish he was dead. How far from God's heart such wishes take you.

This son also left his father's *home*. It's hard work taking the road of unbelief into the far country of exile from the God who loves you. You've got to rid your life of every reminder of him. The boy 'got together all he had' (v.13). He severed every link with home; he left no anchorage or ties with the father's house. He took all his clothes, his tools, his boyhood playthings—everything which might have jogged his mind towards home. The backslider similarly seeks to cut off all connections with God and God's people. He won't have anything around him that reminds him of God. Perhaps, like this boy, you have long since 'set off for a distant country' (v.13) and tried to get as far away as possible from home. You scoot past any Christians which you may meet inadvertently in the street. You never open a Bible. You even switch off *Songs of Praise* on the TV. You're keeping your distance. For lost sons to find God is as difficult as for a thief to find a policeman, and for exactly the same reasons. And so you too, like the prodigal, may be distancing yourself from the Lord just as far as it is humanly possible.

He also left his father's *health and wholeness* by 'squandering his wealth in wild living' (v.13). Out in the far country he rented a plush apartment and lived it up on wild parties, fast chariots, loose women and all the trendy diversions on offer in his day. He had a great deal of fun and pleasure. Sin can be fun. But Satan never made anybody happy, not even for an hour. All the pleasure he had was at the *Father's* expense. Satan, who never even made so much as a blade of grass, can't give pleasure to anyone. That's why there is no pleasure in hell. God is not there. Even the twisted pleasures of sin ultimately come from God. The pleasure of sex is God-given. The pleasure of acquisition is God-given. The pleasure of good food and drink is God-given. The pleasure of being your own boss is also God-given. So when people call sin pleasurable, in a very real sense they are right. Twisted sex, the pursuit of things, the indulgence of appetites, and the philosophy of 'doing your own thing' all carry a certain degree of pleasure with them, but only because they are pale reflections of how God really intends us to live. The boy 'squandered' his living, we're told, because sin's pleasures are both *expensive* and *short-lived*. Sin's returns are very poor. It wastes our money, our bodies, our time and our talents. Sin withers our moral sensitivity, weakens the will, dries up the highest emotions, and paralyses the intellect. It will ultimately ruin us.

That's why Jesus makes clear in verses 14–16 that this son also forfeited his father's *happiness*. The backslider is the most miserable man or woman on earth, if not immediately then sooner or later. 'After he had spent everything, there was a severe famine in that whole country, and he began to be in need' (v.14). He found out that the Bible was right when it says, 'The way of transgressors is hard' (Prov 13:15, Authorized Version). Life without his father began to turn sour. The money ran out and things went wrong all around him. Food was scarce, inflation rocketed prices, jobs were hard to come by, and his 'fair weather', mercenary friends all deserted him. His search for independence and autonomy led to him becoming a drop-out, what Jesus here describes as a *misthios*, or day-labourer, the lowest of three ranks of workers in first-century society. A drifting, shiftless, anxious and uncertain lifestyle which meant existing from hand to mouth, one day at a time.

We've seen how God may chasten his sons to bring them home. Maybe you too have begun to feel the pinch of misery and unhappiness as your months or years in the far country are beginning to pall. This lad had thrown out the sensitivities imparted through his childhood and teenage religion: he was performing the unthinkable role of feeding 'unclean' and despicable swine. He who had chosen to live like a pig now found his new 'home' among them. The exciting and popular Johnny 'Cool' of the mystic East had become plain John Doe squandering his life away as he'd once squandered his Father's money. What a picture of the backslider's true condition!

This is Jesus' moving description of the loss and lifestyle of all who depart from the Father's love and the Father's presence.

Rear Admiral Sir Richard Byrd describes how once, in his distinguished career, he captained a ship which lost its bearings in the cold and dangerous waters of the North Atlantic. His comment on the incident is very moving. Reminiscing about that time he said quite simply, 'I knew I was lost and I felt sick inside.'

Something akin to those emotions began to sweep over the soul of the prodigal son. 'He came to his senses,' said Jesus (v.17). From this we can conclude that it is a type of insanity to wander away from God. Why? Because it is to live far below the potential God created you to fulfil. The road home begins with 'coming to your senses'. Isn't it insane to choose to live in a dusty, spider-infested and leaking outhouse if you are the heir of a mansion, and a suite is already reserved for you in its spacious apartments? Isn't it madness to lock yourself in a prison and so never even begin to realize your full potential in God, let alone enjoy the sunshine of his favour and his presence? Wake up to who you are! Let the masks, the make-up and the pretences fall away, or in short 'come to your senses'. Admit that life without God is not normal, happy or free. It is degraded, miserable and bound. As the boy said, in complete integrity and realism, 'I am starving to death.'

Then, like this young man, you must resolve to go back. 'I will set out and go back to my father' (v.18). 'I'm starving' is hardly the noblest reason to start home, but most people go back to God for no more flattering reason than that they are making a mess of their life without him. God wants you back so much that he'll settle for anything rather than see you excluded. The time to get your motives completely right may come much later. Notice that this lad did admit he'd been wrong, 'I have sinned against heaven and against you' (v.18). We've no reason to doubt that his little prepared speech was sincere. It was genuine repentance. The boy didn't wait for someone to take him home. Ultimately no one will and no one can. It's a decision you'll have to make for yourself. Postponement and wobbling indecisiveness are not good enough. You must resolve to go, and having made your decision, you must actually get up and *go*! 'So he got up and went to his father' (v.20).

He didn't wait to wash. Still stinking of the pig-pen he went home just as he was. He didn't send home a telegram asking for more cash to make him feel good again. He didn't so much want to *feel* good as to be *made* good. So his prayer of repentance shows us a genuine change of heart with no strings attached. He blamed nobody but himself. His rising sense of dignity caused him to feel the freedom of being able to admit both to God and to everyone else that he had hurt, that he was wrong. 'I have sinned against *heaven* and against *you*.' A child once quizzed his mum after she'd cooled down from a particularly bad display of temper tantrums, 'How come when I do anything bad it's because I'm *naughty*, but when you do anything wrong it's because of your *nerves*?' I can answer that. It's because ever since man's fall in Eden, we have all been inveterate blame-shifters.

The prodigal son refused to blame his glands, his biorhythms, his diet or his dad. He simply blamed himself. With no fingers crossed, no return ticket and no lame excuses, he went back to the father who loved him. This is repentance. Or as William Gurnall defined it: 'To forsake sin is to leave it, without any thought of returning again.' The prodigal got out of the pig-pen, left his old companions and his old lifestyle, and went home.

It's fascinating to see just how humbled he had become. He thought that the father would acquiesce in his suggested arrangements and that the most his father's kindness would stretch to would be a job as a hired hand for some indefinite period of probation. 'I am no longer worthy to be called your son; make me like one of your hired men' (v.19).

Instead, Jesus describes for us a wonderful reunion and a thrilling welcome, full of love, tears, new beginnings and even a big party (vv.20–24).

The father actually ran out to meet him—far from dignified for an old man (v.20)! But then God is like that. You and I think he'll never have the likes of us back into the family and own us as his sons. The most we could hope for is a shed at the bottom of the garden. But no. God doesn't stand on his dignity, he runs out to meet us. At the cross God's beloved Son, Jesus, was robbed of all dignity so that you and I could be forgiven. There Jesus was mocked, degraded, spat upon, nailed and crucified in terrifying darkness. God won't 'get even' with you for going astray. He got even with you at the cross. The road back to the Father is stained with blood and tears, and neither of those precious substances are yours. God cares for you and he'll come more than half way to greet you should you decide to return.

The carefully prepared penitent's speech never came out in its entirety (compare verses 18–19 with verse 21). It was interrupted by the father's display of unrestrained emotion as tender arms went around the prodigal's neck and hot, salty tears of welcome and love fell on the shoulders and cheeks of the returning son.

This is how it will be when you come back to the Lord. No rebukes, no recriminations, no 'I told you so' snide remarks. The son who had wished his father was dead now had the past kissed into forgetfulness by that same father he had offended. And far from being made a drudging day labourer in a field far removed from the house, out came the robe, the ring and the new shoes, all symbols of restored honour, renewed authority and ownership, and the revived fortunes of wealth, luxury, freedom and sonship. The Christian life is one of joy, privilege, happiness and surprises.

But more than this, Jesus tells us that the father threw a party (vv.22–24)! Does God throw a party every time a backslider returns? Yes he does! Your wife, your husband, your friends or your workmates may not be so glad to see you come back (remember how miserable the older brother was), but God will be glad, the angels will be glad, God's people will be glad and you will be glad. That being so, I can't think of one reason why you should stay as you are, can you?

Maybe it's time you too got out of the pig-pen and went back to the Lord. So in Jesus' name I ask you: What about it? Are you ready to come home?

Notes

1. Dr D. M. Lloyd-Jones, *Romans: The Final Perseverance of the Saints* (Banner of Truth, 1975), an exposition of chapter 8:17–39, p.318.
2. C. H. Spurgeon, 'New Park Street Pulpit', Vol. 2, Sermon 75.
3. ibid.
4. F. F. Bruce, 'The Epistle to the Hebrews', *New International Commentary on the New Testament* (Eerdmans), p.112.
5. See Greg Haslam, 'You'll get there in the end' in *Chosen for Good* (Kingsway Publications, 1986), pp.131–157.
6. This view is ably advocated by R. T. Kendall in *Once Saved, Always Saved* (Hodder & Stoughton, 1984), pp. 131–137, and all the more interestingly since Dr Kendall seems to have changed his mind over the interpretation of Hebrews 6 in recent years. This book is a very powerful statement of the eternal security of believers, and essential reading for those who are in doubt about that precious doctrine.
7. Which is the condition of all unconverted people. Like Saul of Tarsus, our pre-conversion rebellion against God is carried out in ignorance and unbelief (1 Tim 1:13)

and is for that reason forgivable. This sin is not, for exactly the opposite reason.

8. J. Oswald Sanders, *Men from God's School* (Marshall, Morgan & Scott), p.122.
9. John Hercus, *David* (IVP), p.101.
10. ibid. p.170.
11. ibid. p.172.
12. ibid. p.176.
13. David Prior, *The Message of 1 Corinthians* (IVP, 1985).
14. John White, *The Race* (IVP, 1984), pp.204–205.
15. Tom Houston, *King David* (Marc Europe), p.140.
16. Shakespeare, *Julius Caesar*, Act 2, scene 3.
17. F. W. Krummacher, *Elisha, A Prophet for our Times* (Baker Book House, 1976), p.238.
18. Don Basham, *Can a Christian Have a Demon?* (Whitaker Books, 1971), p.60.
19. R. C. Sproul, *The Holiness of God* (Scripture Press, 1986), p.42.
20. Dale Stone, *Decision Magazine*.

Chosen for Good

by Peter Lewis, Roy Clements and Greg Haslam

Edited by Robert Horn

Three men, endowed with a remarkable gift of teaching, expound the basics of the Christian gospel. Here we see man in his need, in utter degradation and hopelessness. Yet we also see God in his glory, choosing to bring lost men and women back into the light of his presence and showering on them the blessings of eternal life.

In this book we learn—

- — how God sees mankind today
- — what he has decided to do about man's plight
- — the meaning of Christ's death on the cross
- — how we can believe the gospel
- — how we can know God will never let us go

The authors guide us carefully through the theological minefield that has been laid around these great truths, and helpfully apply them to our everyday lives. As such it is ideal not only for new Christians, but for all those who wish to gain a deeper appreciation of what God has done for us in Christ.

Kingsway Publications

One in the Truth

by Robert Amess

'Evangelicalism today is not marked by mutual trust and affection, but rather by distrust, recrimination and animosity,' writes Robert Amess. 'For many, fear is the order of the day. Fear of their constituency and fear of its leaders. Fear of what men might say. Fear of being labelled.'

Robert Amess believes that there is a cancer in Evangelicalism: a love of controversy, a contentious spirit, a party mentality revealed in jealousy of one another's ministry, in boasting and in-fighting.

Yet this is a book not about division but unity. 'Arms of love can and must be stretched out. We must try to understand what others are saying and thinking. It is not necessarily our various positions but rather our attitudes that are offensive to God.'

One in the Truth calls us to repent of our bitterness and anger. It is a cry from the heart for unity.

'His please for unity is not about compromise but holding our distinctives in love . . . Every church leader should read this.'
—**from the Foreword by R T Kendall**

Kingsway Publications